DROPPED IN IT

- by Colin Hall -

the autobiography of a Cotswold Boy and Arnhem veteran.

CONTENTS

My Mother's Funeral

Summer 1988. A Vauxhall Cavalier is racing down the M4. It is driven by my son Alan, aged thirty-nine at the time, and the only passenger is my wife, Joan. They are late. Alan had given himself just two hours to get from Surrey to Weston-super-Mare. I told him he'd need longer, he didn't agree and now they have just minutes to spare. An appointment at the solicitor in the town - Alan waits in the car while Joan goes into the office to sort out the will - we were left a few pounds - there was nothing else, but that's not why they're here.

Back to the car and to the crematorium but they don't know the way, Alan doesn't have a map. The streets all look the same, it's a bigger place than he thought - then Joan spots a hearse.

"Follow them!" she points, "They must be going where we're going."

They join the slow moving queue of cars and arrive as the service begins. The small funeral procession they had been following was the one they had come for. They've made it, just in time.

A few other people are there to say their last goodbye to Marie-Ada. They look at Alan and Joan with a certain degree of malice. Their minds seem to shout, ".....why are *they* here......*we* were her friends.....".

Joan and Alan do not speak to them, there is nothing to say. The service is over and everyone leaves. Alan drives Joan back home. They have spent just twenty minutes there. The others remain for a while, standing around to gossip and the words seem to sting through the air, "....*poor* Marie...........she died alone...........family abandoned her........".

Maybe those other people at the gathering thought that they knew Marie, but I don't think they did. She was *my* mother and I didn't go to her funeral.

CHAPTER 1

My Unusual Beginnings

I should have been a Brummie. My natural birth parents were from Birmingham, from a long line of Midlands folk - the Amphletts, the Benches, Gibbs, Hulberts, Poultons, Boalers and Sumners; all of them born, lived, worked and died in the centre of England, not often even venturing further than the next big town. A century ago people mostly stayed put, not like nowadays where moving two hundred or even two thousand miles away from your place of birth and all the people you know is considered nothing out of the ordinary at all. And I suppose I should have been one of those folk, growing up on the outskirts of some big city, following in the trades of one of my ancestors - perhaps an ironmonger, a grocer, a toolmaker, blacksmith or stockman - any of those trades, living a very usual life with siblings, cousins, second-cousins all around. But my life was thrown a little out of sync from my family and the repetitions of their lives; I was never to become another Bench from Birmingham but a Hall from Herefordshire. The two world wars changed a lot of things of course, but my own circumstances of birth were what removed me from the Midlands and changed my fate just a little. In many ways I still had that 'usual life' of my ancestors and certainly my life is no more remarkable, courageous or exciting than plenty of others - after all many babies are abandoned and many men went to war - but my unique story is to have survived these events and to be able to tell of the details that filled my world for nearly ninety years and to record the incidents and changes that I experienced and witnessed - some dramatic, some very ordinary - but all of them now a part of me and a personal history to be passed on to my own descendants as well anyone interested in a more general history of a life of a working man in the 20th century.

I have researched my family tree, obtaining birth, marriage and death certificates. Parents, grandparents, great-grandparents - as far back as the records at Holborn would take me. When I began looking there was no Internet, it was all done by hand by turning countless pages in the giant books at the records office up in London and visiting libraries and churches for old parish records and, as I have said, my ancestors all were born, lived and died in the Midlands. I seemed to have been the first exception. I was fortunate to grow up away from the growing industrialization of these towns and cities, and live my first twelve years in the beauty of the Cotswolds.

My biological parents met soon after the Great War. My father, born in 1897, was John Lewis Bench (known as Lewis), and in his early twenties he found himself home from the 1914-1918 Great War, lucky to be alive, but suffering from his experiences in the trenches. He'd returned with an injury and minor shell-shock, which was common of many thousands of other young men at the time.

Lewis was relieved that the fighting was over and now wanted to get on with the rest of his life. By 1919 he was fully discharged from the army and was looking for work and looking for love. He wanted to settle down and continue with normality and what he sought was fairly basic - a job, a wife, a home, a family - just the same achievements and comforts that most young men would have wanted.

My mother was called Marie-Ada Amphlett (known as Marie) and was born 1902. She was the daughter of Ada Gibbs who was herself the illegitimate daughter of Sarah Boaler. Sarah had been married twice but had had two children *after* the death of her second husband. She worked as a housekeeper so perhaps the father was one of the staff or even the house owner. These bare facts are never recorded, the birth certificates leave a blank under the column of 'father',but Sarah was lucky to have a live-in job where she could raise her three children and go on to have two more babies. Many single mothers would have had to part with their children, giving them up to the orphanage or face the whole family resigned to the workhouse. The typical Victorian workhouse was a most unpleasant place. They had reputations of accommodation and food not much better than a prison and working conditions so dreadful that they really were a last resort, only one step away from living on the street.

Sarah's youngest daughter Ada grew up with the threat of the workhouse over her and so when she came to have her own children she wanted more for them. Ada believed that her daughter Marie deserved more than a career as a domestic servant, which was a common occupation for working class girls of that era. Ada had higher hopes for Marie and brought her up to be spirited and ambitious hoping that her personality would help her find a better life.

By the time she was seventeen years old Marie Amphlett had already formulated an escape route to take her away from the path that her grandmother, mother and sisters had all endured. Marie considered that she could do better. She had already decided that she wanted more than being told to do someone else's dishes and laundry, sweeping, cleaning, polishing, ironing and a hundred other orders and that the easiest way out was marriage - this would provide some financial support for her while she followed her dreams.

Marie-Ada Amphlett as a child, with her mother Ada Gibbs

Her hunt for a husband brought her the prize of Lewis Bench, age twenty-three. Lewis would have been very happy to put down his roots and live a quiet life after his years in the war which now saw him battle-bruised and stressed from his months of witnessing slaughter on the front-line. My mother, Marie, must have been quite a catch to be able to be lured by Lewis. There were plenty of young women who were unable to find a partner due to the shortage of men after the heavy casualties of the war and it was quite widely accepted at the time that many young women would have to expect to stay single. The whole country had lost millions of eligible men not just in the war, but also from the following flu epidemic and through emigration of those hoping to find a new life abroad in America and Canada.

My father, Lewis, certainly would have had choices, but he chose Marie-Ada Amphlett. Perhaps he fell for her because she was young, healthy and pretty, perhaps because Marie was lively, confident and knew her own mind. Marie was very definitely glamorous, stylish and modern for the age and for her circumstances, and she had ambition too. Marie had an ultimate plan beyond the marriage - she had desires to become an actress. She had some talent for singing and dancing and certainly had a flair for performance. After all, she was easily able to charm Lewis a man five years older and wiser and who, before he had met her, had no notion whatsoever of a career in entertainment. Marie used her charms to the point of being devious and manipulative. She eventually persuaded him to join her in her quest for fame. Although Lewis himself had no talent as an actor, he *was* able to play the piano *and* he could drive. These talents were what had attracted Marie because these were two skills that Marie could utilize for her own gains. Marie wanted to travel abroad, she had very strong aspirations of becoming a professional actress and performer and it is certain that her thoughts were directed to more than just the stages of English musical halls and local theatres. Marie's grand plan was of becoming a film star - the film industry was in its infancy at this time but was growing rapidly, especially across the Atlantic in America and it was to America that Marie looked.

Certain events delayed whatever schemes Marie was hatching. Lewis had suffered emotionally from his time in the war as many young soldiers had, seeing so many deaths and horrific injuries and it left him fatigued and nervous. He suffered from intermittent digestive disorders and what he really needed was a long rest to recuperate. However, he needed to work to earn money to be able to marry Marie and provide for her. There were no disability handouts in the 1920s, every man had to fend for himself or starve. He would happily have found local employment and settled down but Marie was set in her determination to become a star. She hadn't picked the wealthiest of men, obviously, but it must be remembered that there were not so many choices at that time and as Marie's family had been one step away from the workhouse for three generations, to her a man like Lewis was a step up. She needed someone to help her raise the money to get to America and with the shortage of available men, now that she had one beguiled she would not let him get away. If he was reluctant to marry her through lack of savings and a home, then she would make him marry her out of decency - and it didn't take her long.

I was conceived at the end of 1920, only a few months after Marie and Lewis first met. A hasty marriage was arranged for the following March. Unmarried mothers were certainly frowned upon and abortion was illegal, rare and dangerous as well as expensive and so Lewis agreed to become her husband to protect her honour, more than because he was ready and willing. After all, Lewis had always been eager to follow the traditional family path of marriage, house, work, children - and Marie had caught him with such bait. He was getting what he wanted, though perhaps not in his preferred order. The young couple rented rooms in Smethwick, Birmingham and Marie went along with the 'family' scenario for a while, but inside her own mind she still had other plans. The stage roared in her heart so fiercely it over-rode any maternal instinct and her thoughts of making it big across the other side of the world certainly did not include a baby in tow. Times were hard with Lewis in and out of work due to illness and it was easy to turn him to her way of thinking - that her plan of stardom mattered more than a family. Now safely married, Marie was able to convince Lewis that the baby was unimportant, and they would not be able to keep it once it was born. *She* was all he needed.

When the time of my birth came, I almost didn't survive and only by chance and circumstance am I alive today.

Late September 1921, and Marie was ready to have her child. In the weeks leading up to my birth, she and my father had obviously formulated a plan between themselves to dispose of me and keep my disappearance a secret. They hired or borrowed a car, they certainly would not have been able to afford to own one, and drove over sixty miles out of Birmingham while Marie was in labour to arrive at dawn on the banks of a lonely river in Herefordshire. I wish I could say that they drove out there with the intention of leaving me as a newborn baby to be found by strangers but I am quite certain it would have suited Marie to have flung me into the river to be drowned like an unwanted kitten. I believe they had intended going as far as the Bristol channel where my tiny body would never have been found, either swept away in the tides or buried in the wide expanse of mud, and then return home to declare to sympathetic relatives that the baby had been stillborn. This never happened because Marie's labour progressed more rapidly than anticipated and they were forced to stop en route, close to Ross-on-Wye, chancing upon some open land near the river Wye itself.

It was dawn, Marie was in the second stage of labour and the baby's arrival was imminent but there were difficulties with the birth, and Marie was in trouble. Her worried husband, fearing he would now lose Marie too, went for help and the first person he met was Mr Edwin Alfred Hall, the village postman who was up early and out and about on his morning post round walking from country manor to farm to cottage delivering the local mail. He often took the route through some woods and along by the river as a short cut, rather than sticking to the footpaths. And by chance, Mr Edwin Hall was married to the local district nurse and midwife - Mrs Beatrice Lily Hall and so when Edwin faced a distressed Lewis and had Marie's situation explained to him, Edwin knew immediately what to do. Abandoning the mail, he ran home to wake his wife and she returned with him to the riverbank and was able to assist Marie and the baby was delivered safely. That baby was me, born in the early hours of 24th September 1921. The immediate drama was over and Mr and Mrs Hall gave the young couple shelter for some days until Marie regained enough strength to travel home after her arduous labour. Of course being a sensitive woman, Beatrice was able to quickly conclude the true extent of what Marie and Lewis had been planning to do.

Perhaps others wouldn't have been so sympathetic to the Benches. However, very unfortunately for the Halls but quite fortunately for me, Beatrice Hall had previously lost her own baby in childbirth and had been left infertile, unable to ever have another child herself and so was quite desperate for a new baby to mend her grief. I was that baby - born at the right place at the right time after all.

So that is the account of my birth - saved at the last possible moment in the most fitting manner.

I was handed over for adoption shortly afterwards, my birth certificate giving me the name 'Colin Hall Bench'. The 'Bench', of course, was never used by me or my new parents, I was only ever called Colin Hall and brought up by Edwin and Beatrice Hall as their own. It wasn't until I was twelve years old that I came to learn of my 'lucky' arrival into the world.

The Benches returned to Birmingham, where they struggled to save up the fare to America. Lewis was frequently ill, in and out of hospital. At one point he had a major operation, after collapsing in the street, which took two and a half hours to perform and three months for him to recover. Apparently he had been close to death with serious stomach ulcers and it was the emergency operation that saved him. Lewis was quite a drinker and smoker and together with the stress he had suffered in the war, his body had become damaged. This was in 1922, before the routine use of antibiotics, so the operation was quite a hazardous procedure as the risk of after-infection that could not be cured would have been high. He wouldn't have been able to work all that time, needing to rest and recover and so would have had no wages coming in - there was no Social Security Benefit system that is available now, he would have had to survive on savings and hand-outs from family. There were letters between my two sets of parents, the Benches and the Halls, for some months after my birth. The letters from both Marie and Lewis were full of woe - how Lewis was continually ill and so unable to work, how Marie seemed unable to find more than a couple of weeks work that suited her and some promises of money and presents for the baby, which did not arrive. They complained about their poverty frequently stating that the rent was eighteen shillings a week and they could barely earn more than a pound (twenty shillings) between them. These letters take on a begging tone as though the Halls were some sort of charity and they expected them to not only look after the baby they had abandoned but to look after them too and I do feel I ended up with the right parents. Strangely there were several letters from Marie to the Halls trying to persuade them to buy an insurance policy that had been taken out in Lewis's name and for which they could no longer afford the monthly premiums. Marie used Lewis's illness as a way to try to convince the Halls that it would be a good investment as he may well die prematurely and the Halls would then be entitled to a lump sum in pay-out money from the insurance company. My new parents showed no interest in this 'deal' and just as well as Lewis Bench was to eventually outlive them all.

Despite their bad luck and lack of money, the dream of a new life in America remained prominent and after barely a year back in Birmingham, saving pennies and shillings from what little work they accomplished between them, the Benches sold their remaining possessions, including their furniture, to emigrate. They arrived in New York on 1st October 1922 and although there were letters between my two sets of parents for a year or so even after Marie and Lewis landed in America, and further promises of money to help provide for me, communications faded quite soon and only a token amount of money was ever sent (for which Marie asked for a receipt!). Contrary to Marie's hopes for a brighter future, the letters barely changed in tone, for they found life in a strange country not what they had expected and whatever difficulties they had had in England, were transported across the ocean with them. There was a Christmas card bearing the sole message, "This country is not so flourishing as reported" which isn't to my mind particularly seasonal. Maybe it was true, that work was hard to come by, or perhaps Marie and Lewis were just a little too fussy about what they would and wouldn't do. Their aspirations didn't fade, which is to be commended, I suppose, and Lewis eventually worked as a driver, mainly transporting Marie and her new theatre friends around. The only other notable job he had was that he transported the cast of a touring play around. The play was about prisoners of war and was called 'Journey's End' and the actor Hugh Williams had the lead role. Marie went some small way to realizing her dream and found bit parts in various productions, including a version of the famous hit 'No, No, Nanette'. Perhaps after securing that small role, she now felt that she was on her way to achieving success and fame, and Lewis who had never really been a part of this lifetime plan now felt obsolete. Marie and Lewis separated and he soon left America and returned to England alone.

Marie following her dream in America

Lewis went back to his home town of Birmingham and lived there until he died in 1988 aged ninety. Marie later remarried in America. Her new husband was Leo McAndrew and they were wed in Iowa City in 1940. They spent some time in Florida running a garden nursery but Marie's high notions of fame and fortune via the 'big screen' never materialized and when after some twenty years of marriage Leo was unfortunately killed in a road accident the widowed Marie also returned to England, living in Somerset with her sister. Marie died a month before Lewis at the age of eighty-six. Neither of my birth parents had gone on to have more children and nor did my adoptive ones, so I have no brothers or sisters to share my story with. Of the four parents, there is only one descendant and that is me!

****

Back in Herefordshire, I don't suppose that Edwin and Beatrice minded too much about the lack of money or the promised birthday gifts for me that never arrived, as they were kind, loving parents and I am confident that the joy of having a child to care for was reward enough. They brought me up as their natural son and for over a decade I had no inkling of my adoption. My mother never told me anything about my birth parents, she raised me lovingly as she would have done of her own true flesh and blood and I truly believed that I *was* her own. I did, however, know that she had lost a baby before I was born, as she kept an envelope with a lock of hair inside - the only memento of her tragedy. It was many years before I discovered the truth about my birth.

My new dad, Edwin, was a local Cotswolds man, originally from Painswick near Stroud. He now lived close to Ross-on-Wye and that was my home for the first four years of my life, first in a rented house called 'Sunny Bank' in St Weonards, then later to a cottage in Wormelow - both tiny villages. My new dad, Edwin Hall, continued as a postman after the move. The First World War had left him partially disabled with a damaged arm after his time in the South Wales Borderers as a Corporal. He had been shot in the upper left arm and it had not been treated correctly as he had spent some time in a German Prisoner of War camp after being captured in France. He made a friend there, a Frenchman - also a prisoner - and they kept in contact after the war, writing to each other throughout their lives though never meeting again.

My dad's injury had damaged the tendons and nerves leaving his left arm permanently half-clenched and claw-like, but as his legs were fine, the job of postman suited him well as it involved lots of walking. My mum's new job was the care of myself and the family home, her career as a midwife over - as was the case in those days for professional women once married with children.

My memories of those first four years in St Weonards and Wormelow are limited. We had a black fluffy cat called Myth and a little black Pekingese type dog called Nipper, and as an only child I sometimes appreciated the company of the pets. Most of my early days were spent at home with my mum. In the 1920s there were no gadgets around the home to make life easier - no washing machine, or vacuum cleaner and so housework took longer than today and with no fridge or freezer, food had to be bought and cooked daily. My dad grew a few vegetables and kept himself busy in the garden. His wartime experiences had left their scars - although lucky to be alive, he was still suffering both physically and mentally. As a Corporal, and as an Englishman of the twenties, the idea of keeping a 'stiff upper lip' was very evident. He was certainly not a man to show an excess of emotions. I remember him very much as a man who liked to be busy, and he especially liked tending the garden. I think he would have loved to have been a farmer but of course, with his injury, job choices were limited and a full time labouring job would have been impossible.

The small cottage that we lived in at Wormelow was called "Bryngwyn" and it was the gatehouse to the Manor, Bryngwyne House, owned by Sir Reginald Rankin. He would often call in person to collect the rent. I recall him as a kindly man who would bounce me on his knee and tell me funny stories. The Manor house is still there though I believe it is used as a nursing home now.

I also recall the joy of being bought my first ice cream and that memory is still very special. I was just two or three when Mrs Greatorex, the kindly landlady of the Tump Inn, which stood opposite to our home, took a shine to me and lifted me onto the pub counter where I sat, and she handed me a cone filled with ice cream - the most delicious food I had ever tasted! I ate it all up - and to this day ice cream is one of my favourite foods. My other memory is not so happy. I was maybe four by now, and my mother decided that I was old enough to run a little errand and go to the local shop unaccompanied to buy a couple of items.

Mum gave me some coins and a list, carefully placed in an envelope and pushed down inside my pocket. Off I set, I knew the way easily, only a couple of hundred yards, down a track, through a small copse to the village store. But to a four-year old, a walk alone of two hundred yards is an adventure though thick woods and hills and valleys and every moment must be savoured. So of course I mucked about, played in the trees, stamped in the puddles, picked up stones and leaves and generally had fun along the way. When I arrived - I had lost the money. The envelope had fallen from my pocket, perhaps in checking that it was there once too often I had failed to push it back in properly and now it was gone. I re-traced my steps as best I could but as I had not kept to the path it was impossible to know where the envelope could have been dropped. My mother found me and helped search, I remember neighbours helping with the quest, but it was lost for good. There was no scolding though and if my mother was upset or disappointed she hid it well for I have only fond memories of her gentle nature.

The Tump Inn, which I mentioned, is still there today and is said to be haunted and visited regularly by a ghost. I can't say that I ever noticed any supernatural phenomena but it's easy to see how superstition can grow and develop in villages years ago when communications were poor, entertainment was sparse and lack of street lighting meant many long, dark winter nights - many hours of shadows and noises out of sight. We had no electricity in our house, and no gas supply. Our only source of fuel for light and heat was oil which was used sparingly. Many days and nights were spent at a level of discomfort unthought-of these days, but to me it was normal, and I'm happy to say my life back then was quite content.

Beatrice Lily Hall, my adoptive mother

CHAPTER 2

Life in Broadway

Soon after the misfortune with my first solo shopping trip, we moved house. My parents had managed to save enough to afford to buy their own home rather than rent. It cost them £400 which was quite a sum. My parents had some savings but the rest was borrowed by way of a mortgage. There was great excitement as the removal van arrived and was loaded with our furniture and other possessions. Mum and I rode in the van while Dad drove his Triumph motorcycle with Nipper in the sidecar. We travelled fifty miles to Broadway in Worcestershire - an hour's journey today but back then with tracks for roads and a laden van it would certainly have been longer and to me it seemed like a world away. We moved into a small cottage called 'Glenrosa' at the end of the High Street. There were two rooms and a kitchen downstairs and a small attic room upstairs. The house is still there today, though it has been extended and improved considerably since I lived in it.

Anyone who has been to Broadway recently will know that it is beautifully kept with all the original buildings, most of them listed, looking as they were when built. It has more tourists than residents and feels to me more like a museum than a real village. It is clean, tidy and a delightful place to visit. Walking down the high street is almost like walking back in time - but not quite. Besides the obvious addition of a few street signs, a tarmac road and some light traffic - it is the cleanliness that is to me the biggest contrast against the reality of the past. When I lived there in the 1920s there were very few cars about and people relied on horses for transport. Horses to ride, horses to pull carts and wagons, horses at the weekly hunts (though I don't recall ever seeing a fox), horses to pull ploughs or turn the cider presses, and with the horses came the horse-manure and the street was always covered in it! The smell was appalling, especially in the summer. There were flies everywhere. Flypaper was probably the biggest selling item in the hardware store! That is something that is never shown in 'museum' villages such as Broadway today, or indeed in any modern film made about the era, but it was something that was certainly very real when I was a lad. If it was possible for anybody to be flung back in time - the smell is the first thing that they would notice.

Despite that negative point, Broadway provided me with a great childhood of which I have many fond memories.

Dad was able to transfer to a new job within the post office and a new round to work, though similar in that he still delivered all the letters and packets by hand, walking the route each day around the surrounding countryside. Not a great many houses, but a lot of walking including going to the Broadway Tower by way of Fish Hill. He delivered to some grand houses, one of which was lived in by the aunt of the future Queen, Lady Maud Bowes Lyon and another by the actress Mary Robinson known as 'Madame de Navara'. The job was not too difficult and Dad was always home by early afternoon to spend time working on the house or in the garden. We now had the space in our back garden for chickens and room to grow plenty of vegetables and fruit, there was always lots to do.

Edwin Hall (my dad) outside "Glenrosa" in Broadway

At the age of five I started school, which I disliked immensely. It was only ten minutes walk away, past some allotments, in Lime Tree Avenue. My friend Esmor Stokes lived very close to the school on the then new council estate and I would call for him on the way. The school had no policy on uniform, probably not many parents could have afforded one, and I didn't get any homework either. Despite this seemingly relaxed atmosphere, I managed to get into trouble often and received the cane to the hand many times - which was common practise in the '20s and '30s. This punishment seems extremely harsh now and was awarded for minor misdemeanours such as talking in class or being late. I was made to stand with outstretched arm, palm up to await between one and six strokes of the long cane, depending on the severity of the crime. The physical pain was extremely sharp but thankfully short-lived. However, more than that, the memory of the fear, the dread and the nervous anticipation still stays with me today.

I don't remember any subject that I enjoyed at all in the classroom and I was certainly grateful we never got any homework as I can't imagine I would have had any enthusiasm for taking schoolwork home with me. The most memorable event of my school career was when, aged eight, I fell off my chair and hit my head on the radiator. I had to be taken to the doctor and have two stitches put in to patch things up. A more appealing part of the school curriculum was woodwork. We would leave the school building and walk to woodwork classes in a building on the high street, the building is now called Trinity House and is used by a fine art gallery. I remember it being full of drills and vices and benches and the floor littered with sawdust and wood shavings. I enjoyed the woodwork more than other lessons though I can't say that anyone ever suggested I should become a carpenter after seeing my efforts. I do have one relic from my attempted craftwork and that is a small, crude wooden box that I made. I used it to keep my Meccano set in and it has served me over the years as a toolbox and in fact is still in use today, worn and battered but still functional. I did have one flair at school and that was being good at sports - particularly running. Sometimes I got a chance to show off at local fetes where there would be games and events for the children and prizes would be awarded too. Over the years, I won many toy cars, boxes of paints and occasionally some money.

Not too long after starting school, I joined the cub scouts later progressing to the boy scouts. The activities we did there were far more enjoyable to my mind than any academic instruction and we learnt the camping skills of putting up tents, tying knots and outdoor cooking on open fires as well as participating in camping weekends away to Weston Super Mare and Sidmouth which we journeyed to by train. We also enjoyed frequent trips to the swimming pool, travelling there in the back of the local butcher's van. Mr Arnolds, the scoutmaster, had a grocery store in town on the High Street and his friend Mr Robinson, the butcher, was kind enough to let him use his van occasionally for the Scout Group. Motorized road transport was not so available or easy to afford in those days. The van was cold and always smelt of the last load of meat so it wasn't a particularly stylish trip, but it was something we looked forward to enormously. Other boyhood pursuits included exploring the fields and woods nearby looking for mushrooms or apples, the latter being plentiful enough as Broadway was a growing area for cider makers. There was a cider producer close to our house and I would watch the horse walk round and round in circles, dragging the wooden beam that turned the huge stone wheel to crush the apples. As young lads, my friends and I were keen to try out the product and we often had the opportunity, in small doses naturally. The quality of cider production seemed to vary enormously, according to the locals, but perhaps they were just connoisseurs from having so much available. Dad kept a barrel of cider at home, as most households did. We lived next door to a pub, but Dad wasn't a huge drinker despite this or having the cider at home, he always preferred to play darts at the pub rather than get drunk. The surrounding hills were covered in apple trees, the blossom being a spectacular sight in the spring. I believe now that many have been replaced by plastic cloches to grow strawberries. They may produce a great product but it really is not quite such an attractive view.

I received a penny a week pocket money which I would take to the shops and spend on sweets, my favourites were sherbet and liquorice. Shopping could take sometime and while mum chatted at the grocery store as the butter, flour, sugar and other foods were all weighed out individually I would browse through the comics, until it was on to the next shop. There was a grocery store for general food, a greengrocer for fresh fruit and vegetables, and meat was bought from the butcher. Beef was plentiful and cheap as was rabbit, but chicken was quite scarce, compared to today's cheap and plentiful abundance, as there were no battery farms then and so poultry was more expensive to rear. Milk came from the dairy up the other end of the road and I remember the milk always had bits floating on the top which people would not tolerate now but back then it was quite normal and all we knew it was harmless. Butter was bought at the dairy too, we kept it in a special dish that sat in a pool of water - cold water in the summer to stop it melting or going rancid and warm water in the winter to make it more spreadable.

Dad, who was an active member of the community, and on the town's committee, organized a campaign for a Co-op to be opened in Broadway like the one at Evesham. He gained support from many residents but he made himself very unpopular with the local grocer, Mr Arnolds, who was my scoutmaster. Mr Arnolds took his indignation out on me many times, which I thought was unfair as I had no control over Dad's campaign, and he would frequently jibe me at the scout meetings with a chant he had made up:

".....gentleman and skivvy, wants a bit of divvy, come over to the Co-op side.....".

It was a bit embarrassing for a while but I was too young to get involved in the politics of the town so tried to ignore it. Dad always voted Conservative, though he read the Daily Herald, a Labour biased paper, maybe he felt the need to keep informed of what the other side were up to and that's where his Co-op ideas came from. Anyhow, concerning the Co-op, Dad was very determined and eventually got his way, and shopping became a little easier as there was more variety and less need to travel to the bigger towns for groceries at the best prices. And of course there was the 'divvy' - like a loyalty award for using the Co-op.

Each time we shopped we would receive a stamp to our Co-op card and when we collected enough stamps we could claim a gift. I still remember my Co-op card number to this day - 10273!

My mum's job as a housewife was certainly a full time one, besides the daily shopping there was the home to take care of. There were no such things as washing machines or tumble dryers so clothes were washed in a copper boiler and hung out in the garden to dry in summer or propped in front of the fire in the winter. We had a tin bath for washing ourselves; all the water had to be heated on the small stove and carried to the bath either in the kitchen or the living room and then afterwards the bath would be emptied outside. We were lucky enough to have a flushing toilet, not everyone did, though it was in a hut out in the garden, we certainly weren't lucky enough to have an indoor bathroom. There were no vacuum cleaners so the house had to be dusted and swept by hand with broom or dustpan and brush every day. Food was cooked on a small oil burning stove with just two burners and a tiny oven. There were no convenient gadgets like toasters or blenders or dishwashers which are often taken for granted today. A housewife's work around the beginning of the twentieth century certainly was real work. My favourite meal was the Sunday roast which was usually beef. This gave us a supply of dripping for the week which was stored in the larder and we ate it spread onto bread for breakfast or for supper. We always had plenty of vegetables, lots of people grew their own as we did, but there was also no shortage of cheap healthy food in the shops. For breakfast I would sometimes eat a cereal called 'Force' which later was advertised as 'Sunny Jim'. It was just plain wheat flakes and the only available boxed cereal I remember. Today we are spoilt for choice in the supermarket and you can find a whole aisle dedicated to just cereals, aisles that are bigger than the whole of Mr Arnolds' old Broadway grocery store.

As a young boy, I had more freedom then than a lad today. I had my own bicycle which Dad had got cheap as a cast off from the Post Office and so could cycle or walk for miles on my own or with a mate or two. I'd tell Mum I was going out and she'd call out, "Be back for tea!" and off I'd go for hours at a time. There was no fear of crime that I recall and certainly no fear of traffic so it was quite safe for us to roam the surrounding countryside. Many hours were spent with my friend Esmor from school, who was the son of the local coffin maker and undertaker. Esmor's dad had a workshop just across the road from my house and I would often call for him there and see his dad in the progress of soaking large panels of oak to be bent for the sides of coffins. Esmor was one of the cleverer boys in my class and he later went to the Grammar school in Evesham. Sadly, Esmor's mother died and when his father remarried they all moved away soon afterwards and I never saw him again. Shortly before they moved, I was fortunate enough to have my first ever ride in a motor car. It belonged to Esmor's step-mother and was a four seater Austin 7. The new Mrs. Stokes picked us up from choir practice one Sunday and took us for a ride around the town - quite an amazing experience at the time, but taken for granted now. As well as Esmor as a keen companion, I had Roland Tandy, Vernon Kite, Bill Lambley and Charles Ingles as close friends. Charles was a good runner like me, but I think I was faster! We would go out for walks as a little gang of schoolboys and often take Nipper our little dog, or Lady, the fox terrier belonging to Miss Massey who lived opposite, next door to Mr. Stoke's undertaker's business. We'd jog together up to Broadway Tower, a folly commissioned by the Earl of Coventry, where we had a fine view of the area. In fact, I believe you can see over sixty miles covering thirteen different counties from that spot - quite amazing and in those days there was no charge to climb the tower. Sometimes I would take a couple of potatoes in my pocket and my friends and I would make a little campfire in the woods with our boy scouting skills. While the dogs busied themselves chasing rabbits, my friends and I would cook the potatoes for lunch which together with some mushrooms and pinched apples, and if lucky a few wild strawberries, provided us with quite a meal. Sometimes we would see a lorry hurtling down Fish Hill, out of control, its brakes not good enough to keep a hold. Motorised vehicles were still few and far between and any driver new to the area was likely to have a nasty accident if not extremely careful. There are a few tricky bends on that steep hill and even today there is a run-off lane in case of mishaps. Broadway was a great place to grow up and I had a very happy childhood. The freedom to roam around the town and the countryside is something I really am appreciative of now. We had simple toys: yo-yo's, catapults and old car tyres for rolling down the road but mostly we had fun out and about exploring. We saw good things and bad - at the end of summer we would see hundreds, maybe thousands of swallows gathering ready to make their migratory flight to Africa, which was quite a spectacular sight. This was also the time I saw farmers clearing out a barn to get rid of the rats, hitting the poor things on the heads with shovels and piling hundreds of dead creatures into wheelbarrows - all part of country life.

In the shorter days of winter I would play indoors. I read the
Magnet, a magazine for young boys, with tales of the fictional
schoolboy Billy Bunter. I enjoyed completing the competition
crossword in the paper called 'Reynolds News' and would often
send in my answers - I even won a few times. I got fifteen
shillings, quite a sum for a young lad. All reading had to be done
by the light of a candle in the evening as we had no electricity in
our house. Mum's favourite author was Edgar Wallace, but I
stuck to comics. Heating was from a portable Valour oil stove. It
was coloured black and had a handle for carrying from room to
room, it burnt with a yellow flame and was smelly and
inefficient. Later, my parents bought some 'Aladdin' heaters,
which used paraffin and burnt with a blue light. They weren't
quite so unpleasant but I would still wake up on cold winter
mornings to find ice on the insides of the windows. I slept in the
little loft room reached by a set of narrow wooden steps. My
window overlooked the High Street and it was from here one
night that I was awoken by shouting from across the road. I
peered out of my little window and could see a crowd had
gathered and the street lit up by raging flames. The house
opposite (the one my friends and I borrowed the dog for our
walks from) was on fire. I watched as Miss Massey threw open
an upper window and flung out a length of makeshift rope
constructed from sheets knotted together at the corners which
she then proceeded to clamber down. I waited with great
excitement for the fire brigade but they never came. The only
fire fighting equipment in Broadway was a water container and
pump on a barrow which was kept locked up in a shed-type

building farther down the road. The bell, which was accessed by pulling on a rope via a hole in the door, was rung over and over to summon the local volunteers but obviously the members of this unpaid fire-crew were all absent or busy that night so nobody was available to unlock the shed and take out the hand-pulled fire wagon and see to the flames. The nearest proper fire station was in Evesham, they didn't come either. A few neighbours did what they could with buckets of water but the fire blazed away for many hours until it finally burnt itself out. Miss Massey was safe, without injury, and her little dog was safe too, but unfortunately the house was gutted. Looking back, it's quite amazing that there were not more accidental fires considering the frequent use of candles for lighting and paraffin or oil lamps for heating. Miss Massey's was the only one I know of.

By the early thirties, we had electricity in our home. All of Broadway received a supply, the roads were dug and the cables were laid and every house was able to have twenty-four hour lighting at the flick of a switch. I don't recall any other appliances, just a single light hanging from the ceiling in each room - but what a luxury after lamps and candles.

By the late twenties/early thirties, life in Broadway seemed to be becoming busier and faster, partly as I was growing up and partly due to the growth in general within towns between the wars. We would take a train to Cheltenham or a bus to Evesham frequently for shopping trips or Saturday morning cinema - watching the usual black and white movies with stars such as Buster Keeton, Charlie Chaplin, Harold Lloyd, Laurel and

Hardy and of course cowboy films, a favourite for me and my friends at the time. I do remember a great excitement when the first 'all talking picture' was released - 'The Jazz Singer' later followed by 'The Singing Fool' - both with Al Jolson. This was 1928 and something special. After that, the talking movies really took off. With no televisions or radios at home the cinema was a thrill and a very strong draw especially to youngsters like myself.

In 1933, some scenes from the film 'Sorrell and Son' were filmed at Broadway, using the Lygon Arms hotel as 'The Pelican' hotel for the story. I mention this only because it featured the actor Hugh Williams, the same actor that my real father, Lewis Bench, had been driving around in America. This provides a strange link to our lives although of course neither of us knew it at the time. I watched some of the filming taking place after coming home from choir practice and some months later we went as a family to see the film at Evesham cinema.

Sometime in the late 1920s my parents purchased a crystal radio set. This was an amazing piece of technology enabling the family to listen to broadcasts from the BBC without needing electricity - not even a battery. There were classical concerts, documentaries, children's hour, folk songs, news, and other entertainment which came into our very house for free and all self-powered! This was the first time we were able to listen to music regularly - and since those times the growth in music availability has been enormous through record players, cassette tapes, CDs, multiple television and radio channels as well as MP3 players and computer access to any song ever recorded at the touch of a few keystrokes. It's quite remarkable to remember how thrilled we were with our simple crystal set and shared earpiece listening in awe to the crackly sound of the BBC's first productions especially when I say that one of the broadcasts I remember listening to was tap dancing - no pictures remember, just the repetitive sound of many pairs of tapping shoes! A few years later Dad bought a proper radio or 'wireless' as it was called. It was a big wooden box with a built in speaker and looked very grand in comparison to the crystal set.

There was also (though not as varied) music in church. I had been persuaded to join the church choir and every Sunday I would attend the two services, together with my friend Charles, dressed in our smart black and white cassocks to sing hymns and psalms to the congregation. We looked quite angelic but were far from it. Our minds were on other things besides worship and we were always eager to get away and only there because our parents wanted us to be. In the summer we would attend the old church of St Eadburgha, quite a trek down the lane, and in the winter we would attend St Michael's, which was closer to the village. There were other duties as a church boy, one of which was pushing along the bier (a wooden trolley on wheels for carrying coffins) at funerals. This same bier still stands on display at St Eadburgha's Church in Broadway today. The funerals that I attended were those of the unfortunate local children who perished at a time before the widespread use of penicillin and common vaccinations that would nowadays have saved them from illnesses such as meningitis, pneumonia, septicaemia or measles. This attendance at funerals always made me feel sad and a little worried that my parents might die -

probably something that all children think about when growing up, but it was pushed into my mind quite frequently by having to witness these funerals. I found these occasions quite distressing as a young boy but had no choice in the matter as being a choir boy was considered a respectable activity for a boy of my age and my parents were respectable people. Although I should say that getting *me* to attend choir was the extent of their religious activity - they never went to church themselves. I was also made to attend Sunday School at the community hall in Broadway, as if going to school Monday to Friday wasn't enough. We were taught the usual Bible stories, all of which seemed rather far fetched, but at least there was no threat of the cane for not paying attention.

Another respectable pursuit was learning the piano. We had a piano in our home and I was given piano lessons for some time. Like many children of my age both then and now, I always managed to find time for anything other than music practice. This is something I regret now as I expect the countless other young students who give up do too and especially since I now know what a good pianist my biological father was. If I do have some genetic bias towards musical talent, I certainly never utilized it - which is a great shame. The piano teacher was our choir master from the church, himself a very accomplished musician despite being blind. I went to his house for the lessons and he was extremely patient and forgiving of my obvious lack of interest, though he was probably inwardly irritated when I was desperately eager to get away and go to football practice having just joined the local boy's team. I did get to play the piano at a festival in Cheltenham once. It was held at the Winter

Gardens on the Promenade. There was quite an impressive glass building there, similar to the famous Crystal Palace but which sadly like Crystal Palace, no longer exists. My little piano recital was not so impressive. The comment from the judge was "Where is your rhythm boy?"

My only fond memories of church and choir were the Christmas carols that we would perform each year, taking a tour of the local more 'grander' homes collecting money for the church, for example the Bowes Lyon mansion, Madame Nevaro's house and the hotel called the Lygon Arms. We were able to raise quite a decent sum and the choirmaster would always keep half for the church and share out the other half amongst us boys for our efforts. The evening carol singing the week before Christmas was quite a highlight of the season. Christmas in the twenties and thirties was a fairly low-key affair compared to today, I don't remember my parents ever having a Christmas tree of our own in the house, though we had one at school. I received presents from Mum and Dad - the usual stocking filled with nuts and fruit, a few sweets. I had books too and one year was lucky enough to receive a model steam engine, powered by methylated spirits - probably quite a dangerous toy but certainly lots of fun. Another point I should mention is about the generosity of Madame de Nevaro. As well as donating substantially at Christmas, quite often during the summers she would invite the local children to her house for afternoons of croquet on her lawn and swimming in her pool. She had a large house and garden in contrast to the rest of us and it was very exciting for us to play in such lavish surroundings.

At weekends Dad would climb aboard the motorbike and Mum, myself and Nipper the dog would clamber inside the sidecar and we would set out to visit Mum's sister Maud in Much Marcle, some forty miles away. This town is now known most, perhaps, for it being the place where the serial killer Fred West grew up. My Aunt was a school teacher and it is possible that she taught either of Fred's parents in the local school. As the years rolled by, the journey that had once seemed a world away now seemed shorter. My aunt was married to Tom Parkes and they ran a smallholding with vegetables, a cow, some chickens and such. They had three daughters called Rachel, Naomi and Gwen who were all a good few years older than me and spoiled me no end.

Life rolled on, good times and bad. I remember a painful and upsetting tooth extraction by Mr Shovelton the dentist when I was ten, and I remember a wonderful outing to the seaside with my mother. We went by train for a day trip to Bournemouth, the farthest that I had ever travelled at that time and my first view of the sea. I also remember later going on an organised coach trip to London Zoo - the first time that I had visited our capital city. The trip was organized by a lady called Mrs Harrison who ran the local bus company and she also had a few vehicles for hire. I also remember a visit by a travelling Circus to the town. This was a huge event and everyone I knew went to see the performers.

My pleasant childhood was to end soon. Although I had no idea at the time my mum was becoming progressively ill. I certainly hadn't noticed her getting slower and thinner and weaker. Her body had declined gradually but her warmth as my carer, protector and provider had stayed hardy. She had breast cancer, but it had only damaged her physically, while inside herself she was still my mum and that was all that I had seen. Mum was taken by ambulance to Cheltenham hospital and Dad and I went with her. I watched the stretcher carry her into the tall brick hospital building. I watched her disappear as the doors closed. Dad visited her every night, driving to Cheltenham in a car borrowed from Mrs Harrison. She was a good friend of Mum's and was happy to help out. Dad and I drove to the hospital and although I would accompany him as far as the hospital grounds, I was not permitted inside - I don't know if it was hospital policy to exclude children from visiting or if my father didn't want me to see my mother so ill. I would wait alone in the car during the two hours of visiting time and then we would drive back home. Nobody had told me the extent of her illness and I fully believed that she would get better and come home. After waving goodbye to Mum on the day she was admitted, I didn't see her again. I didn't even say goodbye because I didn't know that I should. She was there for a week before she died. My last memory of her alive was seeing her being wheeled on a trolley into the building clutching her brown tin box which she used as a travelling bag. I still have this box today and just one glimpse of it brings the memories gushing back.

The funeral was held at Yatton Church, close to where my mum's sister, my Aunt Maud, lived. Naturally distraught, the day passed in a blur of tears and pained heart. It had all been so sudden. I felt frustration, anger and disbelief. Dad tried his best to offer some comfort and to lessen the loss.

"She wasn't your *real* mum anyway." he said, and told me a brief story of my origins.

This was the first time I had been told about my adoption. The facts brought no comfort, only shock and confusion to add to my grief. Later, the whole saga of my unusual arrival into the world was told to me - Lewis and Marie Bench's midnight drive from Birmingham and how they were forced to stop at Ross-on-Wye where my dad found them and where my life was saved. But I had spent twelve years believing that it was Beatrice who had given birth to me and to find out these strange facts after she was gone shocked me. My dad's attempt to bring solace had been clumsy and cold and had made things worse. I felt only utter confusion and emotional pain.

CHAPTER 3

Living in Croydon

After my mother died, there were many changes to both my life and my dad's. We were of course both still distressed and finding it hard to come to terms with the sudden loss of the lady of the house. Her death affected Dad far more deeply than he dared to show and it seemed he withdrew from his emotions for a while. Far from wanting friends and family around him for comfort he seemed intent on turning them away. While Mum was alive, we had spent many happy weekends at her sister's house in Much Marcle, but now that Mum was gone, the trips were less frequent. The trips stopped altogether when my Mum's mother (Grandma Collins) died soon after. She had left a little bit of money to be shared out amongst her grandchildren but as I had been adopted, I had not been included. My Dad felt that I had been rejected and I suppose he felt that the memory of his wife had been snubbed too and refused to let me visit my aunt, uncle and cousins any more. Dad had some relatives of his own that I had met a few times over the years, there was a brother in Wales, a brother in Hereford, a sister, Annie, in Cheltenham and some cousins there too. But Dad didn't feel inclined in his grief to keep in contact or visit and we lost touch with most of them, though I did meet up with my Aunt Annie and her husband many years later during the war and became friends with them both.

My Dad's loneliness must have been very hard for him to bear because, despite rejecting all support from family, it wasn't long before he decided to advertise for a 'companion'.

He had put a formal advertisement in a newspaper for a paid position as 'housekeeper and companion'. I don't know how many ladies responded, but one afternoon I was given instructions by Dad to meet a 'Miss Alice Froud' at Broadway station and entertain her at the village teashop until he was able to join us after work. Alice had come from Dartford in Kent, where she had been working as a nursing assistant - a similar profession to the one that Mum had followed, so I suppose Dad thought she would be of a similar nature. We were both to learn later that she was not. In the teashop we chatted about her journey, the weather, school and the town and then Alice began asking me lots of questions about my dad. She became quite anxious to learn as much as she could from me about him - his friends, his temperament, his job and in particular how much money he had - it began to feel like an interrogation and I was relieved when Dad arrived to take over.

Alice Froud and Dad came to some arrangement concerning household 'duties' and she soon moved in with us. Over the weeks and months that I knew her I came to like her less and less. It seemed to me that she was a very disagreeable woman, and a very poor substitute for my mum. In a very short space of time, Dad and Alice were married. It was a shock to me and I am not certain whose idea it was initially but I would guess it was Alice's. The future should have looked rosier for us all now as a family, but far from creating a warm and friendly atmosphere in the house Alice seemed to turn herself into a typical fairy-tale 'evil step-mother' character. They were married in the Catholic Church. I did not attend, there being some rule about me having to convert to Catholicism which neither myself nor my dad were keen on and so I was kept well out of the way for that event. As soon as they were married the arguments started. Alice demanded from my dad that I now be put into care, as I wasn't her son and neither was I his real son so neither of them should have to be responsible for me. Dad, naturally, refused completely but it didn't change her mind. I would frequently hear her saying they had to "get rid of the boy" and it certainly didn't warm me to her at all. Alice was impossibly strict with me, whenever we were alone, she would shout at me or clout me if she didn't get her way.

Of course as a grieving twelve year old, no-one could replace my mum and I don't suppose I was ever a perfectly behaved child, but I firmly believe that Alice made no effort to get on with me at all. My own dislike of Alice Froud only deepened as the months passed and I was witness to many arguments between her and my dad - sometimes quite verbally aggressive and on a few occasions physically aggressive too. These were scenes that had never happened between my mum and dad. It seemed to me that Alice would wind up my dad with her nagging and arguing, pushing him into a confrontation at any possible chance. All this constant bickering and arguing provided a background of bitterness which was completely new to me and I did not like it and naturally it only added more stress to my tragic situation. I was still coming to terms with the news that my dearly loved mum was not my natural mother and now that she was gone, not only was I grieving because of her absence but grieving that I had never been given the chance to

45

discuss my origins with her.

There is one particularly nasty memory of Alice that I have which occurred one morning at breakfast. Alice had started a quarrel with me and lost her temper, she whacked me hard and as she raised her hand to beat me again, my dad appeared at the door. He should have been at work, delivering the mail, but for some reason he was home and had caught her red handed in one of her spiteful acts of pure nastiness. There was an almighty row and my dad whacked Alice several times. Things were obviously not working out, and Alice left for a while. Unfortunately, she soon came back.

The domestic atmosphere had changed dramatically in just one short year since my mum's funeral. Alice seemed more uptight than ever now that she was back and there was a constant stress within each of us trying hard not to let the bickering turn to fighting and for a while things were quite uncomfortable. Alice left our house more than once and each time she would take all the money she could find and any other items that might be of value. Dad knew by then that she had only married him for a home and some money, but it was too late - she was his wife and he had to provide for her.

I have only one good memory concerning Alice, and that was the dog that she bought for us to replace Nipper who had by now lived out his life. It was a springer spaniel which we named Buster and I adored him, but on the whole, life with Alice was not so good.

The stress of losing Beatrice had affected my dad severely. He was not a man to talk about feelings - the only emotion acceptable to show to excess was anger, all others were bottled up. The loss of his dearly loved wife, the rejection from her family and the strain of constant quarrels with his new wife made him decide to leave Broadway and try to start a better life elsewhere. By the time I was thirteen he had sold the house and we had moved to Croydon, just south of London. It was a huge move for me, I had grown up in and come to love the Cotswolds and although living near to London did hold some excitement, it would mean leaving my friends, school, neighbours and everything that I knew.

My dad bought a small terraced house in Capri Road at Addiscombe in Croydon. It cost him £620 which he raised by selling the property in Broadway and borrowing the rest. Croydon, which although today is just another suburb of London as is every house in the huge mass of endless houses within the M25, back in the early thirties was a large town in its own right. It had a choice of theatres, a market, cinemas and a big department store called Kennards, which I believe is Alders now and the town was also the home of the largest airport serving London - Croydon Airport, surrounded by fields. All this has now gone, the airport becoming redundant with the development of Heathrow and Gatwick.

We became settled in the new house and after a few months Alice came to live with us once again. I suppose Dad thought he should give the marriage one last go, perhaps Alice would be happier nearer to her own family in the South East. But this time it lasted only weeks - she and my dad continued to argue constantly and with a small further episode of violence (from both parties) she was gone, never to return. I don't know if they ever actually got divorced, though I have a draft of a letter Dad wrote in 1936 to a divorce solicitor. Whether he sent a copy I don't know but the tone of the letter is angry and accusatory, stating that Alice was "...one of those women who marry for a regular income for life..." and that she had tried to claim thirty five shillings a week maintenance from him when she walked out soon after they had married in Broadway. Dad didn't try marriage again, it had been too bad an experience.

After Alice's departure Dad employed a succession of house keepers, none of whom I particularly bonded to but the most memorable being the last one, Gwen Chatfield, an unmarried mother from a nearby hostel who arrived with her young daughter, Janet. I suppose I was glad to have another child in the house. Janet was only about two when she arrived, over ten years younger than me, but as I had just said goodbye to all my school friends and as I had never had a brother or sister, it was nice to have another youngster in the house. Although Gwen always seemed rather grumpy to me, she was a very good cook and she was well educated and her daughter Janet was good company so I was pleased to have them around. My dad got along with Gwen much better than with Alice and although they never married, they stayed together for the rest of his life. Dad had never been afraid of speaking his mind, but it did seem that after Mum died and after the bad experience with his second wife, he became more disagreeable than before and at times could be an awkward character to get along with. He managed to fall out with one set of neighbours in Croydon pretty quickly when he found a dead rat in our garden and threw it over the fence onto next doors lawn. Later that day it arrived back with us, only to be returned by Dad. It was pointless really, but caused an argument that left both sides on non-speaking terms.

Dad was still a keen gardener and grew lots of vegetables in our back garden and he also kept a few chickens which I remember produced the most beautiful eggs. Sometimes one of the hens would become broody and she would be given a china egg to sit on to satisfy her nesting instincts. Dad kept rabbits too for the meat, and he would kill them and skin them himself.

The house was small but comfortable enough. We had electric lighting but no appliances, except for the radio. We certainly had no refrigerator, they were still quite rare, so to keep food fresh for as long as possible we had a cupboard with cold stone slabs and a perforated zinc door (to keep the flies out). We sometimes had the luxury of ice-cream delivered by road in a hand cart by the 'Man from Walls'. He had brass bowls full of the stuff and we would queue up in the street to buy a few scoops, which had to be eaten immediately of course.

I started at the local school, still with my strong dislike of all lessons and now finding that although I was keen at sport, I was no longer the best with so many more boys at this new, bigger school. We had our sports day at Crystal Palace on a proper athletics track and it all seemed very grand compared to the muddy fields I had been used to running on back in Broadway. So, after spending just over one year there, not prevailing at anything, I was more than happy to leave when I reached the age of fourteen. It was considered quite normal and decent for me to finish full time education and start work at this age. While at school I'd had a Saturday job helping out the local baker on his round. I'd meet the baker at 9am on Saturday mornings at the top of the road and he would have with him his van, pulled by a horse called Nobby. This amazing horse, who was old and wise, knew the round by heart, stopping automatically at each of the regular customers' houses. Everyone loved him and he was fed a constant supply of apples, carrots and cakes all morning. I was paid two shillings a week and helped out for about a year. I had enjoyed earning a bit of money for myself in that part-time job and now I was eager to progress to a full-time wage. I didn't take any exams at school so I have no qualifications. That was quite normal in the 1930s, most boys were expected to go on to some sort of manual labour where grades on bits of paper meant nothing.

My father had transferred his employment within the post office and was now working at the sorting office in Croydon and he was able to help find me a job of the same sort. After the depression of the 1930s jobs were harder to come by and so Dad used his connections to get me an interview with the Post Office Headquarters at St Martin le Grand in London and I became a telegraph boy. I was given a smart uniform and bicycle and reported each morning to the local telegraph office with the other boys and young men where we would wait in turn for messages to arrive which we would then have to deliver by hand to local houses. In those days there were very few telephones and so important or urgent messages were delivered via a telegram. The cost was sixpence for ten words, and so as can be imagined many messages were contrived to fit the constraints of six pennies worth of words. Of course I delivered much sad news of family illnesses and deaths but also there were many times when I would be transferring the less serious notes of racing tips, quite often from the nearby Epsom Downs race course. On one occasion I decided to follow one of the tips myself, the encouraging message of "PIGSKIN CAN'T LOSE" tempted me to place a shilling on the horse of that name. He lost, and I didn't bother taking racing tips seriously again.

Me in my Telegraph Boy uniform

My wages were eleven shillings a week and I had plenty to spend it on. A seat at the cinema cost 6d or a shilling, depending on the view. We would see films by Laurel & Hardy and the Crazy Gang. The music halls were similarly priced and I saw Max Miller, Tommy Handley, Flanagan & Allen and George Formby. At fourteen years old I was three years too young to buy alcohol so my drinking career came later and with a pint of beer at only fourpence it took off quite quickly once I reached the legal age, but at just fourteen I *was* able to buy cigarettes and I began smoking, my usual brand was Woodbines at five for tuppence. The heaviest I ever became at smoking was probably fifteen a day. Back then smoking was allowed everywhere - cinemas, theatres, buses, trains, pubs, bars - so it was an easy habit to keep. I'm glad to say I gave up many years ago, with today's restrictions it must be a difficult pastime to enjoy.

I continued in that job as a Telegraph Boy for three and a half years. At sixteen I had progressed from bicycle to motorbike and the Post Office arranged for my road safety training. They also arranged for us younger boys to go to night school two evenings a week to keep up our academic studies. We learnt History and General Knowledge, all paid for by the Post Office. I'd left all my friends in Broadway when I came to Croydon but through school and work I now had new friends and my best mate at that time was Ray Annetts. He was a Telegraph Boy too and we would cycle to night school together. It was here, one November evening in 1936, that we heard news that the famous Crystal Palace Glass Building was on fire. We left the class and cycled over to watch. I'd first seen this huge and impressive building when I had attended my school sports day. It was 135 feet high and over 1800 feet long and now flames and smoke engulfed it. Despite the size and despite over four hundred firemen attending the blaze, it took only a few hours for it to be destroyed beyond repair - helped by the high winds of that night.

My career at the Post Office would have probably continued much longer, even into the years of the Second World War, which was just around the corner, if it were not for a chance happening in the spring of 1939 when I was seventeen and a half. I went for a walk up George Street in Croydon town centre with my friend Ray. We stopped to glance at some very appealing adverts in a shop window asking for new recruits to join the Territorial Army. The posters made it look like fun, it was only part-time - we would still be keeping our day jobs - but we would get to earn a little bit more money on the side too, and it was comparatively well paid, but the most exciting bit was that we would get a free holiday to Folkestone that summer, in August. We both signed up straight away and when Britain declared war on Germany on 3rd September just a few months later, because we were already affiliated to the military, we were forced into becoming full time army employees for the next six years - which was something neither of us had seen in the ad. An impulsive decision to go for a stroll up the shops was to direct the next course of my life.

CHAPTER 4

My War Years in the RASC

Being a member of the Territorial Army meant training some
weekends and some evenings at a local site, usually at the centre
in Poplar Walk in Croydon, right where Marks and Spencer's is
now. I still worked at the telegraph office, delivering the
messages by motorbike all over South London and North Surrey
throughout the week, but when the weekend came, Ray and I
went down to the TA yard, dressed in uniform to train. It was
nothing difficult, it seemed nothing more than being in a grown
up version of the Boy Scouts and getting paid for it. We did
marching up and down the yard and rifle drills - nothing
particularly taxing and a small price to pay for our 'free' holiday.
Ray and I went to Folkestone in late August, it was officially a
training week, but we had plenty of time off to enjoy the sun and
the sea.

We had no inkling of the impending war but obviously the
bosses of the armed forces had, and they'd tempted us in with a
freebie holiday. Now we were stuck - as once we were
employed by the army we were the first to be called up for full
time duties.

I got my call-up notification by telegram on 3rd September 1939
and went straight round to the drill hall. My career at the post
office was over from that moment, I was now a full time soldier.

We didn't stay with the TA though, we both enrolled with the

RASC, a transport regiment as it was better pay and we would get to travel around the country a bit and get to learn how to drive cars, trucks and other vehicles. Being only seventeen (I was a few weeks away from turning eighteen) when war broke out we were too young to be sent abroad - the minimum age at that time was twenty-one and to me that seemed a long time away and war would surely be over by then. The First World War had lasted four years so surely this one would be briefer. We both figured we would have an easy time in the RASC which only seemed to involve driving and it had the added advantage of a regular wage - we would be entering full time employment, earning more than we had as Telegraph Boys and also be seen to be doing our bit for the country. So besides the general unease of war, which everybody in the country felt, we were not too bothered about the situation. Perhaps this seems a little nonchalant but a point to remember is that at this time in history all past generations had experienced at least one major war in their lifetime and would have been involved in some way, whether through personally taking up arms and battling for the country or on the home front experiencing rationing, parting from loved ones or close family members being lost in battle. The end of the Second World War in 1945 was the last time in Britain that that remained true. For over sixty-five years now (more than two generations) we have not had a major war and so peace time with its relative safety and sense of security has become normality.

Soon after joining the RASC our unit was mobilized (prepared for active service). We were given lodgings in civilian houses in Maidstone for a couple of months, living with families and then later we were moved to accommodation at Woolwich Barracks. For me this was quite convenient being not far from my dad's house in Croydon, I was able to jump on a number 54 bus and return home at weekends.

I stayed with the RASC for four years, on a pay of about fourteen shillings a week, until 1943, moving frequently around the country from one barracks to another. First I went to Woolwich, then Maidstone, Feltham, Olympia, Slough, Cheltenham, Chelsea & Victoria, and Doncaster, before my last station at Dover. We would have frequent weekend leaves, obtaining a train pass for travel. I would go back home to Dad and Gwen in Croydon. Ray and I were together until I got to Feltham. He didn't transfer with me, and I didn't see him again until after the end of the war, but I made plenty of new friends. At Maidstone I stayed in another civilian house in Bower Place for a while with an elderly couple. It was during my time at Maidstone that I met Ida Merrils, my first proper girlfriend, but things didn't last too long - with all the moving about with my unit it was hard to keep a relationship going and we both moved on to find other partners. Our time off was often spent ballroom dancing. That was the fashion all over the country then and us blokes would turn up in uniform looking for girls. It was about two shillings entry fee which included a beer and a lemonade. There would maybe be one or two hundred people there so it was easy to get a date. I must have danced with hundreds of girls over the years. When I was at one of the Birmingham dance halls, I met a young lady called Iris Green. We dated for around nine months. I met her parents, from Middlesbrough and she came with me to Croydon to meet Dad but sadly that relationship didn't last either. Things eventually fizzled out and we also went our separate ways.

Me in the RASC

Really I had an easy time in the RASC. It was a good job with secure pay. The war lasted for over five and a half years and for the first five of those, I stayed in England. I was not sent abroad to Europe or the Far East as many men were and so encountered no real fighting or battles. We were, however, issued with uniforms and rifles. There was a period of time in 1940, I think after the retreat of allied troops from Dunkirk, when the threat of invasion from the Germans seemed most likely, and for about a month we were required to carry our rifles with us at all times, even off duty. So as an eighteen year old lad, I would go to the pictures in the evening, complete with loaded rifle slung over my shoulder.

Dad and Gwen did their bit for the war too. Dad, at fifty-six years, was too old for the regular armed forces so he signed up with the Local Defence Volunteers, better known as the Home Guard. He'd had experience of military life in the First World War, so it was no big deal for him to get back into uniform or hold a loaded gun. Gwen was called up to work in a munitions factory co-incidentally alongside the famous entertainer and clown Charlie Cairoli and Janet, still quite young, was sent to Cambridgeshire as an evacuee. She stayed with a lovely family at Newmarket who really took a shine to her and kept in touch years after the war was over. They were even kind enough to leave her some money in a will.

The fear of air raids was high right from the outbreak of war. We had an Andersen shelter in the back garden as many families did. It was a corrugated steel tunnel half sunk in the ground with earth piled on top. It was cold, cramped and prone to damp but made us feel we had a safety hole to bolt to if necessary. Quite often the sirens would sound and people would rush to the shelters. For a few months these were all false alarms and nothing actually happened, and then when real German bombs were dropped (the first ones were on Croydon Airport - so this was very close to home for me) the awful situation of war was made clear as civilians were killed and buildings were destroyed.

One evening I was travelling from Croydon to Slough by bicycle as part of my job, delivering some papers, when an air raid started. When I reached Putney the searchlights had picked out a German Bomber. As I looked up I heard a stick of bombs drop close by. I jumped off the bike, my heart racing, and flung myself flat on the ground - not knowing what else to do. The noise was terrifying and the closest I had yet come to any incident. Although both the bike and I had nothing more than scratches, it was certainly a frightening experience and the first taste for me of real danger. I carried on cycling once the ground had stopped shaking, the rumble of bombers still in the skies, and on reaching Colinbrook on the Great West Road, shrapnel began to drop from our own artillery fire. With sparks bouncing off the road all around me I pedalled as fast as I could trying desperately to avoid the flying debris. I was very grateful to reach my destination physically unscathed though still shaking inside.

I was eighteen by the end of that September and by then I often travelled by bike or motorcycle delivering documents from one war department to another. For six months the following year I also drove a motorcycle daily between Cheltenham and the War Office in London carrying important blue print maps. One night on the return journey to Cheltenham, near a village called Northleach, a chap in overalls flagged me down. It was a British pilot who had made a forced landing. There was an air raid in progress forty miles away at Birmingham at the time and his landing had been a result of that. I gave him a lift on the back of the motorbike to the next village of Andoversford. I dropped him off at the first house we came to with a telephone cable (not many houses had them at that time) so he could call to his HQ to be picked up. I felt as though I had helped out in the war effort with my small deed.

The maximum speed on the Royal Enfield 350cc bike was 70mph, and when travelling back and forth to London this is what I did for most of the way. Going flat out on an empty road was quite a thrill, until the winter set in, then it was cold and uncomfortable and when the War Office decided that I'd need a sidecar to carry all the extra papers they were producing, I told my commander that I couldn't ride with a sidecar and so I was transferred again.

Most or the wartime for me was spent with the RASC and it meant learning to drive - something I would not have done at that age if I had not enrolled. The driving lessons were all included as part of being in the unit, though it was pretty easy work as there were so few cars on the roads back then. I drove coaches and buses of military personnel around the country and I drove lorries with equipment and supplies for other units. I also acted as chauffeur to military officers on occasion. The most notable being the British employed interrogation officers Captain Stokes and Lieutenant Barren, who incidentally was a director of Carrera cigarettes, a big well known company at the time. I didn't like his manner, he seemed very gruff - no doubt well suited to his job of extracting information from German prisoners of war. As there was not much motorised transport about in those days, particularly when the war started, I did feel it was quite a privilege to be where I was. The roads were almost clear of traffic, except for military vehicles. On a typical journey of fifty to a hundred miles I might only see half a dozen cars on the road, far less frustrating than today's congested state. Petrol, amongst many other items, was rationed of course - military vehicles had priority with other services such as tradesmen, for example: butchers, bakers, ironmongers, coming second. There were no motorways and roads were in a poorer state than they are today, and at night all lights were blacked out to avoid buildings being detected by night bombers. The headlights of our vehicle were covered too, except for a tiny slit to let out the minimum of headlight beam and also all of the road signs had been removed as a security precaution - if the enemy invaded it was as well to confuse them as to their exact whereabouts!

Besides trucks and buses I often got the chance to drive some nice cars too. Whilst stationed at one of the London barracks I often got to go to Eaton Square, near the King's Road in Chelsea. Eaton Square was where I would pick up and drop off many army and government officials. The houses there were very grand and had been abandoned temporarily during the war by their wealthy occupants who no doubt had a country retreat or two to shelter in, safely out of the way of bomb threats. Past residents had included British Prime Ministers Stanley Baldwin and Neville Chamberlain, the actress Vivien Leigh and the German Ambassador to London Joachim von Ribbentrop. There was an underground car park just around the corner from there in King's Road (it's still there now but it's used as a car park for a supermarket) where there was a range of flashy vehicles including Humber Pullmans, Humber Snipes as well as the less flashy Ford Prefects and Morris's. I saw Churchill's car with its bullet proof windows, one of my mates had to drive him to Chartwell a couple of times, I didn't ever see him myself though I did drive a few Generals around, which made me feel quite important. As a driver it was my job to maintain the vehicle I was assigned to as well. This included draining off the radiator water each night in cold weather as there was no such thing as antifreeze at that time, I also had to clean the plugs, adjust the gaps, check the oil and tyres and keep the car clean both inside and out - these were all daily tasks and kept us busy. I was at Eaton Square one day when the air raid siren sounded and people ran for cover. A man passed by me and thrust a bulging brown envelope into my hand. I never saw him again as just then a bomb dropped directly outside the entrance to the underground air raid shelter that had been dug out under the gardens in the square. Many people were killed. I helped to move the dead bodies - I was just nineteen and this was the first time I had seen a dead person. All my previous experiences of death had been bodies discretely shut away in sealed coffins. But now I was seeing the lifeless forms of people who up until just moments before had been walking, talking and living their lives just like me but were now killed in an instant and their corpses lying sprawled on the pavement were a shock to me as it brought home the fact that at anytime anyone could have their life wiped out in an flash. I'd had two near misses earlier in the war while on my bike and motorcycle and now this close shave, I was beginning to see the grim reality of war.

The bodies from incidents such as this were often taken to Streatham Ice rink for temporary storage as it was a large cold place ideal as a makeshift mortuary. It was a morbid sight to see rows of corpses laid out on the ice waiting for collection by grieving relatives. After the clearing up was done after the Eaton Square bombing, I remembered the envelope that had been shoved into my possession, imagine my surprise when I found it to be full of pornographic photographs. My mates and I got much entertainment from that. We'd never seen anything like it - dirty pictures were not so common as today!

I'm second row from bottom, fourth in from right

Dover was my final station as a member of the RASC. I was sent there in early 1943. Dover was very lively with dogfights in the air and shipping being shelled frequently. It was known as Hellfire Corner; being only just over twenty miles away from occupied France it was the most accessible town for the German forces to target. The town was always heavy with troops. My job at that time was to drive an ambulance and call on the local gun sights and a medical centre under the castle. The Germans used to shell Dover most nights and cinemas and theatres were closed although the pubs stayed open - we needed some relief! The bloke in charge of us was called Sergeant Major Vigour. I hadn't got off to a very good start with him as when we first met in his office he caught me laughing at his wedding photo. I don't remember what was so funny, probably nothing, but as lads we liked to fool around. Vigour must have taken offence and seemed to be forever on our backs after that. Some of it we brought on ourselves, for example, we had a mate whose surname was 'Crow' and when Vigour called him across the yard, 'Crow! Crow!' we would imitate him shouting out 'Caw! Caw!' He caught us and, again, wasn't too happy. I got into trouble another time, when I was driving an ambulance. The old vehicles had a horn in the steering wheel, which was a cylindrical device that could be lifted in and out of the centre of the wheel. The driver before me had put a sign under the horn for a laugh saying 'Nosey bastard!' Vigour managed to find this too and thought it had been directed at him, and I got the blame. He also caught me smoking in a vehicle. We all smoked, all the time, even officers smoked, but I was unlucky enough to get caught and he confined me to barracks for two days.

During my time at Dover I'd made some good friends in the RASC. My best mate was a bloke called Tommy Farrage. He'd been a professional footballer before the war playing for Gateshead who were in the third division, and he still played whenever possible during the war for our regiment team. We got into a few scrapes, the most regrettable was when we went out poaching. Meat was short in the war and we knew there were some deer on an estate in the area. We rather fancied a nice bit of venison so we took our rifles and shot one, chopped off the legs and took it back to share with our mates. We didn't get caught but we didn't enjoy our kill either. The deer didn't die instantly and we had to finish it off with a blow to the head. Besides that, it was tougher meat that we'd thought and we wasted much of it.

Tommy and I were both becoming fed up with the constant shelling of the town from across the channel, the closure of the cinemas, the crowded pubs as well as our misfortunes with Sergeant Major Vigour, so we decided to volunteer for a different unit. We chose the Parachute Regiment. One of the attractions of this regiment was the promised fourteen days leave after our initial training. We also thought it would be more interesting than listening to artillery every night and besides that, it was extra pay. We were accepted in May 1943 and sent for training first to Hardwick Hall in Chesterfield, where we spent about twelve months and then later to Manchester and then to Leicester. It was vigorous training and I became the fittest that I had ever been or have been since. We had physical training every day including climbing rocks, crawling through water, carrying a man on our backs for a hundred yards, climbing ropes using only our hands and arms - no legs, and boxing three rounds with each other as well as training on various weapons such as Bren guns - assembling, firing, disassembling and cleaning. I spent more than a year in the regiment before we were posted abroad. We came close a few times. In June 1944 there were the Normandy landings - 'D-Day'. We expected to go and attended several briefs, but at the last moment were not needed and so stayed on, safe in Leicester. During those months of training we had visits from the king, George VI and Field Marshal Montgomery. I suppose we were supposed to feel honoured that they had come to give us 'pep talks' in person, but to us lads they seemed very artificial, especially when Montgomery told us how proud he was of all of us - after all, he didn't know a single one of us personally of what our motives were. To me and Tommy, it was just a paid job that we'd gone into to get away from the bombing in Dover. It could have been any job, we certainly weren't looking for honour or glory and for him to assume a proudness over us didn't quite fit.

Besides our ground training we also had specific parachute jump training. The first couple of jumps were from a barrage balloon and the rest from an aeroplane called a Whitley Bomber. For our first jumps from the balloon we were taught briefly how to land then we were kitted out. Our parachutes were made from green nylon and re-used again and again and were folded back into their packs by the women in the WAAF, and before we knew it we were up in the balloon which was held in place on a long cable. It went about 500ft up and we jumped one at a time, our parachutes opened automatically for us by way of a rip-cord as we left the basket. Sometimes, depending on the wind, we would swing violently from side to side and if we hit the ground on a downward swing it didn't half hurt! There was a rule that we could refuse any of the first eight jumps and drop out and not suffer any disgrace, but after eight jumps we were officially in and any refusal after that would result in 150 days detention. I'm happy to say that I didn't refuse any, despite knocking my chin badly from my first aeroplane jump. The jumps were made from a hatch in the floor of the plane. The hatch was opened, we leapt out feet first. Sometimes the slipstream would catch the jumper's legs and thrust the upper body forwards resulting in a bashed face on the edge of the hatch. It was a common problem and even had a name; it was called 'Ringing the Bell'. I did just that on my first attempt and needed three stitches to my chin.

It didn't put me off, and I continued with the practice. After each jump we would gather back together - sometimes the men were spread miles apart after jumping singly from the plane and so it would take sometime to re-assemble, then we'd have a cup of tea in Tatton Park in Cheshire, ten miles away from Manchester Ringway Airport, then back to barracks. There were plenty of other lads who got similar knocks and the resultant blemish to the chin was named a 'Ringway Scar'. Tommy and I passed all the jumps and the training and got our 'Wings' to become full members of the Parachute Regiment.

I enjoyed my time in the regiment. I was with a great crowd of blokes and we were given plenty of free time and allowed out every night to the town. We spent the time boozing and dancing with the local girls who shared their attentions with the

American forces also based in the area. We were encouraged to enjoy our leisure time, there were lorries each evening to take us to and from Leicester. Some nights, Tommy, some other mates and I would be so drunk we would miss the ride home. My friend Harry Sanbrook had struck up a deal with the local air-raid shelter minder. He was a retired man who didn't mind accepting a few small bribes to give us a roof for the night. We called it our hotel and the warder loved playing hotel receptionist and even supplied an exercise book for signing in and out. Harry would always use the name George Grables (pronounced Grey Balls) as he thought this amusing.

The training was tough but within our limits and the conditions were reasonable. We always had decent meals, maybe basic foods like corned beef and mash but always plenty of it, we always had enough fags and we always managed to find beer at any pub we went to. There was rationing of course, and many civilians went without cigarettes and beer but the pub landlords would always hold some back for men in uniform. Everything was fine except that now we were fully trained we felt we didn't get enough leave. When our training had ended we'd had a whole fourteen days leave and I'd spent mine back in Croydon with Dad and Gwen. Funnily enough it was during that leave that I had bumped into my old commanding officer, Sergeant Major Vigour, the man who I thought had given me such a hard time in Dover. He was very pleasant to me and asked how things were going and told me I looked well. We had a good chat and he told me my old unit with the RASC had recently been transferred to Croydon so if I'd stayed with them instead of joining the Parachute Regiment I would be back home every night. I couldn't believe my bad luck and resentment certainly began to build up inside me.

We were all used to getting weekends off to go back home to our families or go out and have a good time. But now things were changing. During the beginning of 1944, when D-Day was being planned and executed, training had intensified and most leave had been cancelled. As I said, we almost got sent on the D-Day landings but our calling was cancelled at the last moment, it seemed the allied forces were advancing in Europe faster than planned and we weren't needed. That happened a couple of times more on other missions, but we always had to be ready to go and so were not allowed any days off. It remained that way throughout the summer and we began to feel hard done by. It was during that summer that my friends Bill Myle and Harry and myself decided to take an unauthorised holiday - go "AWOL" as it was called (Absent Without Leave).

We knew from our time in the area that both Manchester and Leicester were full of military police and so decided to take our break in Oldham. There were no troops based there. We left early morning taking the bus and then train. On arrival we booked ourselves into the local branch of the YMCA - a hostel for young men. We were still in uniform, but nobody ever asked us who we were or where we had come from - I suppose a man in uniform had a certain respect and if anybody believed we were up to no good, they certainly never reported us. We soon found jobs at a brewery called the Pallentine Bottling Company shifting crates and barrels about, easy work for three fit young men. After a couple of days we made friends with a generous lady named Mrs. West and her daughter who then rented out their spare room to us. There were other servicemen working in the area - Canadians, English, soldiers, sailors - it seemed we had found a den of hideaways.

We went out most nights drinking. Our favourite pubs were 'The Grapes' and 'The Top Drum' and another one called 'Help the Poor Struggler'. This last one was once run by Albert Pierpoint, better known as the last hangman in Britain. He must have had a sense of humour for in the pub was a sign saying 'No hanging around in the bar'. It was after one of these nights out that our vacation came to an end. I got so plastered one night (we often started the evening a little tipsy after sneaking a few drinks at the brewery day job) that I wandered off out of the pub to find the gents and became lost. I came across an empty air-raid shelter and being shattered by then decided to sleep there for the night, hoping by morning I could remember where I was! I staggered inside and took off my trousers rolled them up for a pillow and settled down to sleep. Several hours later, just before dawn, I needed the loo again and I tottered outside. I'd chosen my time badly for just at that moment a policeman was passing on his nightly rounds and he immediately arrested me for, I presume, indecent exposure - I was still minus my trousers. I spent the following day in Oldham jail. I was unable to be released, even after I'd sobered up as I'd left half my uniform behind at the shelter. Eventually, the Quarter Master at Oldham Military Pay Corp was able to send me some trousers and I was released. There was no charge from the police but now that the military had been involved I felt no option but to go back to my unit. It was now September 6th, 1944. I had been absent for twelve days, during which time my Dad had been contacted and asked if he knew of my whereabouts. He, of course had no idea where I was, I had not been in touch. Very soon, my Dad would have no idea where I was again, but next time he would believe me dead.

My friends gave themselves up too and we were each sentenced to twenty-eight days in the army prison for our absence. I may have got more, but my commander, a Captain C M Horsfall, had written a reference of good character on my behalf calling my past standards of behaviour "exemplary".

My time in the army prison was not an enjoyable experience, at least not after the delights of twelve days freedom without responsibility. The prison was a converted stable block. The cells were the stable stalls, each one sleeping five men. There were about twenty men in there at any one time. The toilet facilities were a block away and we had to be escorted to and from them when needed. There was little to do all day except sit around and read and smoke and talk. The food was the same as the other soldiers who were not inside the prison, which was a relief because mealtimes were the highlight of the day after the seemingly endless boredom.

I did not get to serve my twenty-eight days, I was there for less than half of that. As I sat flicking cigarette butts at the wall, Whitehall was busy planning a mission to further advance the allied troops in Europe. Unknown to me or Harry or Bill we would soon have our jail sentences cut short and would be on our way to Holland to take part in "Operation Market Garden".

Me as a new recruit to the Parachute Regiment

CHAPTER 5

Arnhem, Operation Market Garden

The war in Europe had been going on for five years now. That was a big chunk out of a twenty-two year old's life and longer than any of us had expected - it was longer than the first world war and I suppose everybody with a memory of those times compared it to that. In retrospect, it is more obvious that the war was slowly drawing to an end, with the Normandy landings in June 1944 and the advancement of the allied troops north into Belgium and southern Holland but there were a few last battles to be won before the German forces were driven out of the occupied zones completely, and until peace was declared, a cloud of insecurity still hovered over the country.

The objective of 'Operation Market Garden' was to free three bridges over rivers in Holland and in doing so enable a path for allied troops to run a safe route for armies already advancing from the south to enter Germany and so end the war. It was instigated by the British forces leader Montgomery, the US forces leader Eisenhower and the Polish commander Major-General Sosabowski. The number of men to be dropped was approximately 35,000. These men came mainly from British, American and Polish forces. They were to be landed by parachute (20,000) and gliders (15,000). As well as the men, there would be much equipment landing too including jeeps, armoured vehicles, artillery pieces, ammunition, food and other supplies.

On paper, the plan must have seemed formidable with such numbers of men and weapons, but in reality, the operation was a disaster and over 26,000 people were killed in less than two weeks because of this battle. The approximate figures are 12,000 British and Polish military men, 4000 American military men, 8500 German military men and 500 Dutch civilians of men, women and children.

By my point of view, and with hindsight, the main reason for British failure was the allied forces underestimation of German strength in the area. We were all told it would be an easy operation. We were even told that the German troops left in Holland were full of 'old boys' and 'inexperienced youngsters'. I'd never been abroad before and I'd never fired a gun at an enemy before. I believed that it would be easy as I had no reason not to accept what the superior officers told us. My mates in the unit and I all did. We were not afraid or even apprehensive, we thought it would be easy because that is what we were told and had no knowledge or experience of our own to contradict them or to make us fearful. If we could have all seen clearly into the future at that point through some magical crystal ball or the like, I guess there might have been thousands of deserters in an instant.

We were in the 1st Airborne division, 10th Battalion and our particular mission was to free the bridge at Arnhem, this was the bridge furthest north and over the river called the Neder Rhine. We flew in low over a coastline previously flooded by Germans to prevent invasion from the ground on September 18th. The plane that I was in was a Dakota as were most of the others, there were gliders too pulled along over the English Channel and then released close to position so they could land with us men who parachuted down. We received a few near misses from anti-aircraft fire, but arrived safely above our target landing area and then one after another, thousands in all, we jumped out of our aircraft to parachute down. We were some sixty-five miles within the German occupied territory. We dropped at Ginkel Heath, near woods, at 2pm without any opposition at all. The quiet was almost enough to dispel any apprehension that had grown within us after getting shot at in the sky. There are 400 men to a Battalion which was split into four companies - A, B, D and HQ. I was in D company together with the other ninety-nine men that I had trained with for months back in England. We all knew each other pretty well having spent so much time on the practice firing ranges, running cross country and drinking together on our hours off duty. As well as regular training, many of us had had specialist training for example as snipers, or with mortar guns, or as medics. My specialist training was as a radio operator in order to keep up the contact within the unit as well as with other units and divisions. I'd been given this job almost on a whim back in England during our training. One day we'd gone out as a unit to practice being soldiers and when the radio we had with us started buzzing I was the only one bold enough to answer it. Although we'd all had the same lecture on radio jargon and codes and the like, I suppose the others couldn't be bothered or felt daft or whatever, but as I was the one who picked up the receiver and used the correct language, my platoon commander, MacKenzie, decided that I was most suited to be radio operator. Other men had to be snipers or handle mortar guns, so I guess I was lucky. The radios we trained with back in England were pretty heavy together with their huge batteries so they weren't much joy to be encumbered with, except at night, because I could pick up music on various radio stations so I'd listen to it in bed. But in Arnhem, we had much lighter weight equipment, so then I was glad of my special job.

Now, ahead of us, we had an eight mile march together - just another day, so we thought. I remember the day before we left England, the girls in the barracks café (it was called the NAAFI, pronounced "Naffy" - they served cheap cake and teas) had cried for us as they waved goodbye, and we had shrugged it off as no big deal, so certain were we that we'd all be home in a few days at the most. We were heading for the town of Arnhem, to help secure the bridge. About 750 of our men had already got through and were to hold their place for the advancing armies from the south. We were aiming to reinforce their position but the Germans had closed in around them and they had been left stranded. They held out for many days near the bridge, led by Major Frost, but they never received the help that was expected. After three days 250 wounded were evacuated and after another day the remainder finally ran out of ammunition and were forced to surrender, by which time their numbers were depleted to about one hundred men. The rest were killed. We should have been with them on the second or third day, but we never arrived. The closer we marched, the more dangerous it became. We were, of course, in the midst of the enemy. The north of Holland was still very much an occupied area and there were German troops everywhere, with more arriving daily. Also, what we were not aware of at the time but were told about after the war was that of the hundreds of planes and gliders that had flown us here, a few had crashed, and in one of the wreckages had been plans of the whole Operation. These plans and maps had been found by the enemy. And as for the 'old boys' we had been expecting to encounter, what we were actually to face were tough SS Panzer troops, with reinforcements sent in from Germany especially for our arrival.

The first day we were there, we saw many Spitfires circling above. They were there to offer some protection to our advance and even though we saw some German anti-aircraft guns take a few shots at them we didn't see any come down. Although far away, they gave off a large puff of black smoke which could be seen from quite a distance. The first night we stayed in the woods. Each member of our battalion had landed with a rifle, a supply of 200 rounds of ammo, some dried food rations such as porridge, minced beef, dried cabbage, a flask of water, some cigarettes and 100 Dutch guilders especially printed by the British authorities (perhaps they thought we could buy souvenirs! Unfortunately I didn't get a chance to spend any of mine), a tube of morphia for pain relief, some M & B tablets for infection (useless, as I later found out) and a digging tool. With this makeshift spade (it wasn't particularly efficient) we dug ourselves mini trenches. There were two men to each trench. We would dig into the soil and pile up the earth at the front, trying to build up a wall of protection to hide behind. We slept there too, though not much - the ground was cold and damp that autumn and we soon became wet, muddy and uncomfortable. Also keeping us awake was the sound of gunfire in the distance and every few minutes the sight of German flares bleaching out the night sky. But we were all young and fit so a loss of one night's sleep was not so bad. I suppose many of us hoped it would all be over by the time we reached Arnhem the next day, which we had been led to believe it would. We assumed that the presence of so many allied troops would be enough to scare off any opposition and the men who landed the day before would have cleared a path for us. I was half expecting not to have to use my rifle at all.

We were not allowed to smoke once it got dark as it was thought that the glow of burning tobacco would give away our position. Many of us ignored that, still believing that the 'war' was something others were dealing with and we pulled down our tin hats over our face and hid the lighted cigarettes under our pulled down jacket sleeves.

The next morning at first light we carried on our approach, marching along the road by the railway line to Wolfheze. Earlier troops had left a trail of German bodies along the route. I'd seen dead men before - clearing up after air raids back in England. These corpses, however, were more battered and bloodied, torn by bullets. Their uniforms a reminder that we were soldiers just like them. The caution in our minds now turned to fear. For me and many of my mates it was a first real sight of the bloodiness of war and how real the threat of death was for us all. We didn't see any British dead, though there must have been some. I believe that all the casualties from our side had been cleared away - not just out of respect but also so that our morale was kept high - like saying "only the enemy get killed, us lot will all be OK". We walked on, silently quaking inside. There was a sudden burst of gunfire and in our nervous state we all threw ourselves into the roadside ditch. Fortunately, that time, it was only one of our own men giving an accidental burst of fire from the cheap and crude sten gun he had been issued with. They had no safety catches and accidents were frequent. We had a laugh about that, thankful that it wasn't the enemy, although I don't suppose the bloke who got shot in the ankle from another sten when the man behind him tripped found it so amusing. Many of our guns were leftovers from the First World War thirty years ago. My own rifle was a Lee Enfield - it had a wooden body and a crude sight on the end of the barrel, no more than a little "V" shaped bit of metal in which to pick out your target and I'd been issued with just 200 cartridges, in effect 200 bullet shots at the enemy - certainly no match for the German tanks we were yet to meet. I remember the sound of the sten guns on our side was a "d-d-d-d-d" as the rounds fired, compared to the German guns which went "WHOOSH". They apparently had a gun that fired so fast and hard it could cut down a tree. Our confidence was not inspired.

The noise of rifles, machine guns, mortars and tanks firing in the distance became louder and more frequent. It wasn't too long before the next close round of fire was obviously coming from the enemy and directed at us. Quickly we dived for cover and started to dig our trenches again. From our hiding position we could clearly see a German tank just a small way along the road. I shared my trench with Bill Myal. The firing increased to a full scale attack. From the quiet of our parachute landing in a field less than twenty-four hours before we were now completely in the thick of a raging battle. Mortars exploded all around us, the Germans would fire a batch of six mortars off then pause, then another six, and another, and another. It seemed they were relentless. Much of the ammunition fired at us hit the trees but much of it hit our men too. We had only rifles with our limited supply of 200 shots each which were running out fast and anyway pretty useless against the tanks and large artillery of the Germans. I saw many men killed that day. A lot of them didn't die instantly but lay screaming in agony from vicious open wounds until eventually they bled to death. There were body parts scattered around. My most vivid memory of that day and the following few days is not the noise or the blood but seeing the dead faces of my mates lying around me. We'd trained together for months and had all become great friends - and now they were gone and each of us left standing knew that any second we could be lying next to them.

My specialised training, as I mentioned, was radio operator. It was my duty to relay commands to other members of our unit and other units such as 'move forward' or 'over to the left'. It was while performing this task on a walkie talkie type radio that I got injured. I lifted my arm as I extended the telescopic aerial on the small radio and of course, my arm was immediately exposed out of the trench. In an instant I was shot through the forearm. My arm now dangled uselessly by my side, blood gushing out. There must have been pain, but the shock and the turmoil of what was going on around me masked that for some time. However, with all the blood and a useless arm, I was ordered to retreat for medical attention. Our medics from the 10th battalion were positioned approximately 100 yards back. Bill volunteered to accompany me. I could have made it on my own but Bill was eager to get away from the front line as much as anyone, so he came too. They gave me a dressing from their limited supplies, but because my right arm was now unusable, I could no longer fire my rifle. I took out the bolt and chucked it away disposing of the now useless rifle elsewhere, as I had been trained to do. I gave my remaining ammunition to Bill and he returned back to the rest of our men. The medics sent me to a house not far away to the south, that they were occupying, to see another doctor. I could no longer defend myself or operate the radio so although otherwise fit, I was basically just a passenger of little use on the fighting front and had to keep out of the way. It was while I was at this house that I saw the Polish gliders shot from the skies. The Germans, as I now know but did not know then, had the plans and maps of the whole operation. They were expecting the arrival of the Poles. They were able to fire at them before they landed, many of the gliders were hit and destroyed in the air. Many men were killed, many more were injured. It was around this time that some of our men fired on the Poles too. The sight of the grey uniforms had them confused. It was a tragic sight and there was nothing that we could do but watch the horrific slaughter from our makeshift hospital. The Germans gained confidence and with a further push, drove our men back further south towards Oosterbeek.

Plenty of supplies were dropped by the allies during this time. There was further ammunition, which we desperately needed, more food and the planes were even able to drop mini motorbikes that folded out of the canisters, but because our mission had been such a disaster and we were not positioned where we were supposed to be, the supplies including the ammunition and food and water were now landing behind enemy lines. I'm sure the Germans were grateful for the help, enjoying our chocolate and cigarettes all the more for knowing that they were meant for us. The battalion was now under-equipped, hungry, thirsty and in serious trouble. The supplies were being flung out of planes by members of the RASC, the very same section that Tommy and I had belonged to before we joined the Parachute Regiment. If we had stuck it out in Dover, instead of signing up to this lot, that would have been our job right now and we'd have flown in, pushed a few canisters out the plane and flown back home and never landed in Holland at all. Funny how little decisions can change your life!

At the house the doctor, who was now the only person there with me, gave me sweet tea to drink which was gratefully gulped down. He received a message that we were gradually being surrounded and so we both made back along the railway line. Others were taking the same route and I managed to jump onto the bonnet of a jeep, sharing the space with a basketful of carrier pigeons. Our journey ended at Oosterbeek crossroads, were the remnants of my battalion were seeking refuge.

Our only remaining officer at Oosterbeek crossroads was Colonel Smyth. My only previous encounter with him was when I had marched passed him shortly after landing at Ginkel Heath and he had caught my eye and shouted across to me "Put that fag out!"

News of my mates was scarce, but heavy losses were reported. Of the four hundred men I had landed with, less than seventy were left to counter the German fire - the rest were dead, missing or seriously wounded including my mate Tommy Farrage. I never saw him again after the first day's gunfire. The present Roll of Honour states him as dying on 20th September but there is no marked grave for him though he is mentioned at Groesbeek Memorial at the Canadian War Cemetery. Neither his family nor I will ever know the details and there are still to this day *many* dead men without officially marked graves. There was no time then for mourning. We were shelled and fired at constantly for around 100 hours. The noise never stopped for longer than a minute or two, the days and nights blending into one long agonising nightmare. Contrary to our previous very laid back state of mind we were now seriously frightened for our own lives. Having seen so many colleagues killed and seriously wounded all we could do was hope for reinforcements. In fact we still genuinely believed that we would be relieved. After all, 35,000 of us had landed to relieve the three bridges with 12,000 of us concentrating on Arnhem *and* our armies were supposedly fast approaching from the south. What we didn't know was that those armies from the south had also been slowed down through lack of supplies - they were still more than thirty miles away and we were still many miles within German lines.

It was a grim time. We were just young men who would much rather be back at home, drinking, dating and living normal lives. We had been thrust into the defence of Europe which, although an honourable and worthy activity, was not our choice. Neither I nor any of my mates wanted to be there. I saw no cowardice but I saw no heroics either. We were there almost on false information (remember, we believed there would be no opposition) and we did what we did because we had to to stay alive - but all of us would rather *not* have been there. Heroism is a choice, we had none.

Without a gun, there was nothing I could do but watch. Our remaining men were enclosed within a two mile perimeter with Germans to three sides and the river to the south. Those with serious wounds such as missing limbs, missing eyes, severe head injuries etc were in three big houses on the crossroads being used as makeshift infirmaries, the rest of us were scattered in whatever shelter we could find.

Most of my time at the Oosterbeek crossroads was spent hiding in an abandoned garage. At least I hadn't had to dig a trench for the night so it was dry, but still chilly. Sometimes I had the chance to dash across the street to get news from the other men and try to get the dressing on my arm changed but there were more serious injuries to attend to, men who were close to death, so I had to make do. Mostly during those terrifying hours we all stayed put. I'd entered the garage by chance when ordered to find cover, now I had plenty of time to look around. There was an old bus in there, up on blocks, unused because of the petrol shortages. A couple of other blokes that I didn't know from other companies were there. They were also injured but they had guns and so a better chance than I should we have German soldiers come too close, but I was still unarmed. I spent most of the time slumped in the corner - tired, hungry, cold and miserable but there was nothing I could do. It was while I was hiding out in that garage that the retreat began. There was a plan to evacuate our troops across the river in boats and head south. Only the fit could go, about 2000 from various battalions in the surrounding area went. My injury meant that I had to stay as there was no way I would be able to swim should I have to. Actually, I wasn't even told about the evacuation, I only found out about it later, after the war. For those of us that remained at Oosterbeek there was plenty of shelling from the Germans, many of the surrounding buildings were hit. Colonel Smyth, our commanding officer, was fatally injured in one from falling rubble.

Sometime later we heard the rumble of a tank approaching. I thought it might be one of ours, but of course it was German. I watched from my hiding place as our men shot their rifles at the heavily armoured tank. The bullets bounced off. We had an artillery gun too, it did no better, and even our shells were no match. We were in a hopeless situation. As the Germans advanced towards us they were searching each building and taking the men as prisoners. It wasn't long before they reached the garage where I was. I'd entered the garage from the front not realising there was no back door, just a small window to the rear which was too high to reach in my injured state as I could not climb up and so I had no chance to escape. Looking back it was a daft place to take shelter, but it was something I hadn't thought of when entering the garage - that I might need to get out quick. Two Germans armed with machine guns entered and as I was unarmed, I immediately surrendered, flinging my hands in the air and crying "Kamerad! Kamerad!" (Meaning 'comrade' or 'friend') hoping they would see me as just a soldier like them and my words would be able to touch their hearts and morals. Others would shout "Frau und Kinder!" ('Wife and children!') in their bid for sympathy.

Naturally, I assumed I would be shot. I had heard that men at one of the houses across the road had been executed, and I'd witnessed many deaths in the last few days. The terror in my mind was immense. But, after they searched us and took whatever food, cigarettes, watches, jewellery we had, they just arrested us, stuck to whatever 'rules of war' applied and we were led out to the street to join the band of other prisoners. There were just thirty of us left in Oosterbeek from a battalion of four hundred. Some had escaped, most were killed. So many others who had parachuted into that quiet field a few days before would never return. It was only after the war had ended that I found out the true extent of losses from all sides involved. Many, many men that I had served with had now gone. I heard that Colonel Smyth had died, as had Captain Horsfell (the officer who had spoken up for my good character when I had gone AWOL in the summer of 1944), the captain of my division, Captain Queripol, had died also, and the lives of many friends were taken too - Tommy Farrage, Paddy Winters, Corporal McDonald, Jim Morris and many more.

I was lucky, all I lost, besides the temporary use of my arm, was a few fags, a pipe and a ring that the soldiers who arrested me had nicked. Small prices for my life.

CHAPTER 6

Captured

The arrest came with mixed feelings. Relief, of course, that we were no longer in the heat of a battle and glad to be out of the way of mortars and shells and also that we no longer had to shoot at others, but anxiety too. Our fate now lay completely with our captors - the very men we had moments before been trying to kill. Naturally, as we walked out of the garage into the open air, our hands raised in surrender we were all still very much on edge, wondering if we were yet to be shot at any moment. We knew that prisoners of war could be seen as a nuisance because they had to be fed and guarded and so took up valuable manpower and we were unsure if the German army could spare the resources. Most of us were in a pretty shabby state from our days and nights in dugout trenches and of course many of us were injured, including myself. The mental and physical exhaustion was very apparent but none of us wanted to die, we still had the will to survive and so were careful to obey and not to antagonise those men holding us prisoner.

The German soldiers who arrested us, took us at gunpoint down the street to behind one of their tanks and we hung around outside while more prisoners were taken. For about ten minutes we actually came under fire from our own side. They were aiming at the Germans of course, but we all had to duck down behind the tank and dodge a few shots before we were safely out of the way. A group of about thirty of us were taken along the road to an old school house. I saw one of the German soldiers kick one of our men up the backside while an elderly Dutch woman who had been watching from a doorway shouted some obscenity at him. I thought the German soldier would retaliate and was quite worried for her, but thankfully he ignored her words. We were taken to a school building, our hands all the time firmly on our heads - or those that could manage, those with injured arms like me were excused this of course. As we walked through the streets there was a German reporter and a news-reel cameraman taking photos and filming us, it would be good news in Germany that a battle had been won and they were keen to show the people their first victory for many months.

We were all terribly tired and hungry - we'd had no proper sleep or food for many days, some of the group had been short of water too. At the school there was a Dutch man, a civilian, and he came around to each of us in turn giving us spoonfuls of stewed apple. It wasn't much at all, not really more than a taste and didn't fill our hungry bellies one bit, but I remember his kindness which was brought about, I suppose, because he felt some compassion for us for trying to free his country, even though our troops had actually failed quite miserably, and he wanted to help out and that bowl of stewed apple was all he had. We were certainly very grateful.

After sometime, the wounded were picked out from the group and bundled onto a lorry and driven to the Queen Elizabeth hospital. This included me, because of my arm. It wasn't a long journey, but at this time, none of us knew what would happen to us and any time we were moved there was always the worry that we had been selected to be shot. On arrival at the hospital I was shocked to see hundreds of men already there, not just in beds but lying in the corridors, and on the stairs. It wasn't just British and Poles at the hospital as I had expected, there were plenty of German wounded too. Most men there were far worse off than me with more serious injuries. There were a lot of amputees and head injuries, some of the men were obviously dying. My bullet through the forearm seemed minor in comparison, but despite this I was given a bed. The hospital was run by a Dutch doctor and I believe he gave me priority over some of the Germans. I slept there that night. I was also able to chat to some of our men and discuss our experiences. A Sergeant Moses from Leeds was there, he had been shot in the knee and was unable to walk. I had noticed that the hospital rooms were unguarded. We were free to move around and there wasn't even a guard on the entrance outside. Being still so worried about our fate now that we were in enemy hands I whispered to the Sergeant.

"We could walk out of here."

Sergeant Moses pointed to his leg.

"My knee's a bit bad." he said.

I hadn't considered that an escape would be impossible for most of the men here and as I didn't fancy my chances on my own I stayed put. Safety in numbers, I figured.

There was still the sound of bombs and gunfire in the distance but I presumed that the hospital would be safe from attack and I was able to rest. If I had been foolish enough to venture outside,

I'm sure I would have been shot. I was now in an area very much controlled by Germans and the few remaining British and Polish men at Oosterbeek that I would have run to were soon to be captured too.

The next morning I was moved again, this time further north to some barracks in Apeldoorn that were being used as a temporary prison. The fittest of us were taken by bus, the trip was about ten miles and along the way we saw the destruction that had happened in the last few days. Buildings were shattered, lots of them no more than a pile of rubble and what was left was torn and tattered. Apparently only 150 buildings remained intact in Arnhem after the war out of the thousands there had once been. Many Dutch civilians had been killed, and of those still alive, the ones that were able to leave had gone and the rest remained in hiding only to be forced out of the town later by the Germans. 96,000 Dutch people were eventually forced to go from their homes, some went to Veluwe some to Groningen. It was a very hard time for many families seeing their town destroyed and then having to leave what remained behind with no place to live and no food or money.

At Apeldoorn, again there were hundreds of wounded men. My injury was checked and assessed and although operations were performed there, my injury wasn't considered severe enough to be a priority and it was just patched up as best they could and given a new dressing. Once at Apeldoorn, I heard no more guns, if the fighting was still going on it was far away. But I did not feel entirely safe, I was well into enemy territory now. My birthday had just passed and of course it went unnoticed to those around me, but I was aware of turning twenty-three and having no control over my future and not knowing if I would ever make it to twenty-four.

I was fit enough to travel so I was moved again, arriving at Lingen prison which was well within German borders. It had been a civilian prison, but was now full of war prisoners. There were plenty of medical staff here and so my arm was looked at again. After having my arm X-rayed by two German nuns, and finding out that the ulna was shattered, some Canadian doctors working for the Red Cross there decided to do what they could to realign the ends of the bone. My arm was still in a mess and becoming extremely painful and by now oozing pus as well. Some rubber tubes were attached to the injury to drain off the pus and then the doctors operated to set things back in place. I would say they did a great job. Although it was painful and took a long time to finally heal, and today (66 years later) I have a huge scar and my arm bones are a little out of place, my arm functions well and I am extremely fortunate compared to so many of the others who were injured far more seriously than me. I stayed at Lingen for two days, then together with a huge crowd of fellow prisoners, we were put aboard cattle trucks and taken by rail to our final destination as prisoners of war, the Stalag XI-B prison at Fallingbostel, Germany.

Fallingbostel was less than one hundred miles away but we had no idea where we were going at that time or how long it would take. Again, the intense uncertainty of our destiny haunted us both night and day. The train went very slowly and stopped frequently with long stationary periods so it took us many days to get there. We were crammed into the cattle trucks, maybe fifty or a hundred men in each. There were Russians, Polish, French, Indians, Slavs and Americans as well as British. There was no room to lie down, we were forced to stand or at best squat. We were given no food and very little water. Some men, I've heard since, drank their own urine to survive. I was luckier in that the train driver had managed to pass along some water from the engine's boiler for some of the men in the first few trucks. One of the stops was at Bremen and at just the same time as a British air-raid. The sentries on the train and station all scarpered and we were left locked in the wagons hoping we wouldn't get hit. How tragic that would have been to be wiped out by friendly-fire at this point. Thankfully it passed and we were left unscathed.

The train was very long with many wagons, trucks and carriages - maybe twenty or thirty, I didn't count. After a couple of days we pulled in to some sidings to off-load a bunch of Russians who were being transported as part of a prison labour force and it was here, when we stopped, that some of the injured, myself included, were selected and taken out of the wagon to sit in one of the carriages.

I don't know why this happened, maybe they needed to empty a cattle truck for some real cattle! But it suited me fine. At last I had a comfortable seat and a chance for food too. At the next stop, while the sentries were out on the platform chatting up the local girls, I crept over to the luggage rack and pulled down a package belonging to one of the guards and inside it I found a large piece of cooked sausage. Naturally, suffering from uncomfortable hunger pains, I ate it. It was the next day before the theft was discovered and an extremely angry German officer stormed up and down the carriage asking who the thief was. I was terrified not just for myself but for all of the other prisoners too, imagining we would all be shot for my crime and so I owned up. Amazingly, I was not punished and to this day I cannot believe how lucky I was. The officer just walked away and never mentioned it again. I can only guess that something distracted him and he forgot. Some of the Germans spoke English but when they spoke only German it all went over my head, so I have no idea what saved me that time.

Two days and nights later we were at the station in Fallingbostel and taken to our designated prison - Stalag XI-B. As we marched into the camp I felt some relief that I had made it this far. I would rather have been home, but prison was better than being dead and I knew that if I stuck it out, I'd be home when the war ended. I didn't know when the end would be - days, weeks, months or maybe years, but I had a chance here, probably a greater chance than on the frontline. To my utter surprise, as I walked through the gates, I saw a familiar face. My friend Harry, who had gone AWOL with Bill and me from Leicester just a month ago, was there waving at me, he had arrived the day before. I was so relieved that at least one of my mates was still alive, he had a small injury to his face where a piece of shrapnel had struck but he was otherwise alright.

As I said, entering the prison was almost a relief after the last week of bombs and bullets, of deaths and injuries. I'd seen many prisoner of war camps in England when I'd been a driver with the RASC. The prisons in Britain housed Germans and Italians and I'd always felt they were treated very reasonably. No-one wants to be imprisoned but at least they had good food and shelter and were out of danger. If I'd known that Stalag XI-B was not at all the same as an English prison for POWs I wouldn't have felt so relaxed. The next six months would show me just how different things were on the other side.

CHAPTER 7

Prisoner of War

At the prison camp, we were put in various barracks, separated by nationality. We were given our prison number - mine was 117616. It's funny that I can remember this after so many years, along with my army service number - 83656, and my Co-op dividend number from Broadway - 10273. These three figures stay in my head while current phone numbers are forgotten as soon as heard.

So I was back with my mate Harry as well as a load of other British men who had also been at Arnhem and Oosterbeek. In the other huts were Canadians, Poles, Russians and Norwegians. Our issued uniforms for Operation Market Garden had included some escape equipment. This was all probably more for morale than actual use. One of the jacket buttons had a compass to show north, we had some Dutch currency (Guilder notes) and we had maps printed on silk sewn into the lining of our clothes. The Germans were wise to this and confiscated all of it. During the time I was in the prison, a few men did try to escape. Most of them were shot. There was a German Barracks opposite Stalag XI-B so there was no shortage of enemy eyes to keep a watch on us, though I was told that one or two got away - but how far they got I do not know.

Soon after I arrived, I was handed a form by one of our men and told to fill it out and hand it back to an officer named Gerry Strachen by 2pm. The forms were to be passed on to the British authorities to report our capture and imprisonment so that our families back home would be aware that we were still alive. I am right-handed but I struggled on the best I could with my left hand, my right still being broken, infected and useless due to my injury but I missed the deadline. Shortly after 2pm I took my completed paper back to Gerry Strachen but being an old soldier and obviously deciding that my unpunctuality showed lack of discipline and I needed to be punished, he screwed up the form and threw it away. My details were never passed on to anyone and my poor dad back home in Croydon never received news of me for the rest of the war all because of this man's lack of thought. For almost seven months I was missing and for most of that time Dad supposed I was dead, although when we eventually met up again he told me that he would tune in his radio each night listening for broadcasts from Switzerland where the Red Cross would sometimes read out names of men that had been traced, whether dead or alive. Dad never heard my name and as much as he didn't want to, he believed that I had been killed in action, my body lost or destroyed. Strachen left the camp before me, he was moved to another one and I was pleased. His quest for a little bit of power in this tragic situation was out of place.

Not all officers were the same. We had another one, Sergeant Major Lord, who would make us turn up for a parade each day to take a roll call and would make sure we kept ourselves and our accommodation as clean as possible. Firmly but fairly he kept good order and even the German guards respected him. Conditions in the prison were pretty grim and a little order and routine helped to move the days along.

No. 3/AAC/1/3   Army Form B. 104—80B.

(If replying, please quote above No.)

A.A.C., A.C.C.,
AND G.S.C.,
6 MAR 1945
RECORD OFFICE,
EDINBURGH, 7.

Record Office,

19

SIR ~~OR MADAM~~,

With reference to previous notification I have to inform you that a report has been received from the War Office to the effect that (No.) *83656*

(Rank) *Private*

(Name) *HALL . Colin*

(Regiment) **ARMY AIR CORPS**

is ~~now~~ at *Stalag XIB (in German hands) Prisoner of War number 117616 and is now known to have been wounded — gunshot wound right forearm. Report states 'Healing well.'*

Any further information received in this office as to his condition or progress will be at once notified to you.

I am,

SIR ~~OR MADAM~~,

Your obedient Servant,

a/uequires D.C.O.

~~for~~ Officer in charge of Records.

IMPORTANT.—Any change of address should be immediately notified to this Office.

(55827) M22108/1261 500m. P.&G. 9/39 52—4094   Forms B104-80a/4

The first news my dad had that I was still alive

97

There was a major lack of food. Each day we had a bowl of watery sauerkraut soup, a slice of bread cut from a loaf divided carefully into ten and if we were lucky, some potato peelings. The bread was divided with as much meticulous precision as could be managed by one man and then the pieces, now laid out in a line, would be numbered from one to ten running from one end to another. The men would draw numbers from a hat and take the piece corresponding to the number. This was to ensure a randomness to the distribution that was as close to fairness as we could get so that no-body could say someone else had grabbed a bigger piece than them. The soup, was most foul and would turn our stomachs, the first few times we had it we were completely unable to eat any. On our first few days at the camp we actually gave away our soup to some Russian prisoners who were reaching through the wire fence from another barracks desperate to get at our rations. They were dirty, scruffy and behaving in a very undignified way, so we thought, and we couldn't understand how they could be so keen to get their hands on this vile slop. I have to admit that when I first saw them I found their behaviour quite pathetic. It was just a few weeks later, when we became as starving as them and willing to eat almost anything, that I then understood their desperation and found more sympathy towards them and even found myself eager to be the one who would fetch the soup from the kitchen, delivered in buckets, hoping to get a little bit extra for myself.

Anything we were able to acquire on top of the daily ration was an absolute luxury. Some of these men had been prisoners either at this camp or others since near to the beginning of the war which amounted to over four years with conditions worsening all the time as the war progressed in the allies favour and German supplies decreased. Occasionally there would be a parcel from the Red Cross, with such things as bread, coffee, powdered milk or cigarettes. Many parcels never reached us, the Germans were hungry too, the war had brought many shortages for them and they took much of the food that was meant for us. The German guards were made up of an assortment of men. They hadn't stationed their best soldiers in the prison camps, there were a lot of old blokes and a lot of injured men there - men with one eye, men with limps, men who were best off right out of the way of the front line and serving elsewhere. Under other circumstances we would have seen them as nice, friendly and ordinary blokes like us. There were a few nasty guards, but then there were some men on our side too who were far from perfect. I didn't have any personal grudges against the 'enemy' and I still don't, and I believe most of us felt the same. We were all trapped in this awful situation, governed by politicians and generals and power hungry nutters, who were themselves living their lives quite comfortably elsewhere.

During my time serving in Holland and throughout my time at the prison camp, I made many new friends. Some of them, sadly, I never heard from again after the war and I can only assume that they perished in battle or later from their wounds. One of these men was a fella called Titch Freeman. He was a sergeant who'd had the misfortune to be too close to a mortar bomb when it dropped. His body was full of shrapnel and his pain kept him awake at night, sometimes he would be screaming for what seemed like hours on end. There were many men in intense pain. Wounds they had suffered during the previous week's battle would not heal both from lack of adequate treatment and from lack of decent nutrition. There was a bloke who had been shot through the ear, the bullet passing down into his shoulder and out of his backside, there were many head injuries, men with arms or legs blown off, ears missing, blinded, bullet wounds and shrapnel wounds. All we had were some paper bandages and some peroxide. With the infected wounds leaking pus, these paper bandages would fall off almost straight away but due to shortages in the prison, once treated, we were not allowed back to the medics for three days to receive another dressing. There was no penicillin or any other type of antibiotic. All we had were a few remaining M & B tablets, some that we had been issued with and some acquired from field orderlies. They were supposed to stop infection but they didn't. I also heard that a side effect of these tablets was depression. Not exactly what any of us needed right then. It was impossible to keep these wounds clean and the stench of decaying flesh hung in the air. Many men died in the camp from their wounds. After suffering the horrors of the battles it was pitiful to see men drop and die through lack of medical treatment. There seemed to be one or more burials every week. The graves were dug in the prison grounds by the other inmates and a short ceremony would be held. None of us knew how long the war would go on and all of us wondered if we would be the next man to fill a grave.

The prison was already overcrowded when I arrived. In the day time we could go outside into the yard (behind fences and barbed wire, and under the watch of armed German sentries) but at night we were confined to the huts. There were about fifty men to a hut with the beds arranged in three tier bunks a couple of feet apart. Already full, these bunks were pushed up closer together and more brought in. New prisoners arrived constantly, the greatest intake was after the 'Battle of the Bulge' of December 1944 to January 1945. During and after this, many Americans were captured and brought in to Stalag XI-B, adding to the numbers. Some were pushed into our hut and after that, we slept two to a bed end to end and had to crawl in to find our place. We were given one blanket each. It was a very cold winter, a famously cold one in fact, and as more men arrived, there was less food to go around. Many men perished in those cold months. More graves.

We stayed in the same clothes the whole time I was there, the same uniforms that we had worn as we parachuted into Holland. These clothes were now sweaty, dirty, torn and bloodied. My jacket was ripped to the shoulder where my arm had been shot and tended to. By the end of the war, my shirt was sleeveless and the rest of it no more than a rag. The only time we took our uniforms off was to be de-loused. This happened maybe two or three times during my seven month stay. The body lice and the bed bugs plagued us constantly. They made us itch, they left rashes of irritating red spots over our bodies. For de-lousing we would undress leaving our clothes in a pile then walk through a room with a spray of insecticide, our clothes were treated similarly. Then we would dress and return to our beds where we would immediately be bitten again by the bugs that crawled out of the crevices of the wooden bunks where they hid. Our same clothes that were returned were minus the adult lice but still contained scores of eggs which soon hatched out to infect us again. Sometimes we would catch live lice on our clothes, their bodies would be bloated full of our blood and we'd catch them then squeeze them dead or take a splinter of burning wood from the stove and crack the eggs open. It didn't do much to keep the numbers down but I suppose it was something to relieve the boredom.

We were unable to wash because we did not have enough water. We didn't need to shave, thankfully, because our whiskers never grew due to lack of nutrition, our fingernails stopped growing too. We couldn't clean our teeth, but soon we didn't need to because most of them fell out.

We had a role call twice a day, outside in the yard we would all stand in rows and be counted. It could take a long time, especially if there was a man short. We called the guard "Fumpf" because of the German number five that sounded funny to us.

Sometimes there would be a chance to leave the camp for the day, under heavy guard of course, either by being selected or volunteering for a working party. Not everybody had the chance, mainly the fit were taken and with my bad arm I was able to go only a few times. The working parties laboured in salt mines, sugar factories, some went to collect wood and some to mend roads. It was hard physical work and not something any of us were really fit for with our lack of nutrition but some of the blokes chose to go as they saw it as an opportunity to maybe get there hands on something to eat - perhaps a swede, a potato or a mangle-wurzel that they might be able to snitch from a field that they would pass on the route. Sometimes a guard would call out

"Get me one too." The times that I went it was once to collect fire wood from the woods and once to help out with road building - all I could manage that time was lifting bricks into a wheelbarrow one at a time with my left hand, and I only went as it meant seeing some greenery for a change of scene. I found the work exhausting, we all did. There was one other excursion for me, and that was a trip on a horse and cart to the station to fetch something for the guards. I went with Harry and a couple of Germans. When we stopped, one of the guards took out a lump of stale bread that must have been at least two months old, to give to the horse. We begged the guard to let us have it, we were that hungry. He gave it to us and we thought it the best meal we'd had in a long time.

The guards, quite evidently, were living a hard life too. They had little food themselves and in particular no real coffee and no cigarettes. If we were lucky enough to obtain an intact Red Cross parcel with these items we would trade them for more bread. Another trading system we had organised was with the new arrivals to the camp. Harry and I and a mate called Bernard Shaughnessy would give the perimeter guards a couple of fags to let us into another barracks where we'd do a bit of trading. We'd swap two loaves for a watch then take the watch to another compound, maybe the French one, and swap it for three maybe four loaves. (These unfortunate new inmates hadn't yet realised the value of food here in Stalag.) Then we'd take our bread back to our hut and swap the loaves for real coffee or more fags, or maybe tins of powdered milk. A couple of times we were fortunate enough to get some tins of meat from a Red Cross parcel. We'd trade with our own men or with the guards if they'd recently acquired one of our parcels. Our little business came to an end one day when Harry, Bernie and I woke to find our stash had been pinched. The whole lot had gone in the night, stolen by another inmate. We got permission from Sergeant Major Lord to search the barracks but we found nothing. It was long gone - traded off amongst other men and lost to us. There was a lot of swapping, exchanging and bartering like this all the time. It all went around and came around and we probably didn't end up with any more than if the whole lot was shared out equally in the first place, but to trade felt like we were doing something positive for our own survival in such dire conditions to convince ourselves that our position was less than the hopeless end that it seemed.

There were other incidents concerning the theft of food. Some men would save their daily slices of bread for the next day, and at night others would creep around and try and steal any saved food. Sometimes men would wail when they found their precious slice of bread gone, it was sad to hear and see men act in such a pathetic manner, but this is what slow starvation was doing to us. We all had to keep watch on our food as it was the most precious thing we had, even though by today's British standards, we were living on a pitiful supply of scraps and throwaways.

The German guards were lenient to our trading practices because they understood our predicament and they didn't want to be there either. We were physical prisoners kept inside by locks, barbed wire and guns but they were prisoners too, in a way. They had no way to escape their jobs and the poor day to day living conditions - the cold and the hunger - other than by desertion which would probably have meant facing a firing squad if caught. Some guards didn't handle the strain as well as others. We were out in the yard one day when there was an air raid, it was British planes up in the skies and us prisoners naturally felt glad and cheered. The guards ordered us back inside as it wasn't seen to be good for them that our morale should be lifted. One of the prisoners, a British glider pilot, was slower returning to barracks than the rest of us - his punishment was to be shot and killed. In an instant, a fellow inmate was wiped out by a burst of anger from a guard. All the individual incidents like this come back to me time and time again, we all felt sick inside that our mate could die for something so trivial.

As the months progressed, the frequency of air traffic from home intensified. We began to hear bombers overhead most days and assumed things were going our way, but we had no real news - just heresay. New prisoners would bring snippets of information, but who amongst us soldiers could say when a World War would end? It was still an indefinite wait not knowing if, with our weakened bodies and our weakened morale, we would find the strength to hold out.

There were other terrible deaths too. There were a few prisoners at the camp that we would call 'bomb happy', it meant that their brains had been damaged in the war from bullets or shrapnel or other injuries and they were now so severely brain damaged as to be no longer in possession of a normal mentality, some of them so bad they were unable to look after themselves on a day to day basis. One such bloke, with a head injury, was unable to keep himself clean and after some time he had maggots in the wound in his head and the nickname of 'Dingleberry' because of his lack of personal hygiene. He was blissfully unaware of his predicament but there was a British Sergeant Major who had little understanding or sympathy for this man and when he saw the state of the man's open wound and how filthy he was he became angry and actually beat up this poor man. One day out in the yard, he laid into him so hard and persistently that some other blokes had to call him off. The Sergeant Major was unrepentant and turned to them snarling "You want some as well?" Eventually he was stopped and the other guys fetched some water and chucked it over the unfortunate victim to try and clean him up, this was after they had stripped him, they then tried to scrub him down. They were trying to help but he was not much more than a skeleton and by now extremely frightened at his ordeal. He ran across the camp and slipped into a ditch and we never saw him again. We were ordered back inside, unable to help him. He either died of starvation or from his wounds or perhaps executed, I don't know which.

Obviously, there were very few laughs at Stalag XI-B prison camp, but many of the inmates tried their best to keep everyone's spirits up. We had a Russian inmate who had been an opera singer before the war and he would often serenade us, he even got extra bread from the guards, it seemed they enjoyed it too. There were a few British blokes who could do a turn or two, a bit of singing, dancing, tell a few jokes. We'd have little cabaret nights. It was something to look forward to and something for those performing to concentrate on as they rehearsed in the days leading up to these entertainment evenings. Not everyone was talented, though they may have had aspirations. In particular, there was an incident when a Red Cross parcel arrived. There was always great excitement when we got our hands on these parcels as it meant some extra food that we all so desperately needed. A crowd of us gathered round as the parcel was unwrapped only to have our hopes dashed as we saw that some misguided dim-wit at the Red Cross had assumed we'd rather have a piano accordion than some decent grub. We all walked away dragging our feet, but a bloke called Jock Muir took hold of the instrument and claimed it as his own - well, no-one else wanted it. Only trouble was, he couldn't play. He'd make a lot of noise, quite frequently, but nothing very tuneful. In fact some of it was ear-splittingly awful. One day, after a particularly long and painful session of screeches and whines, he called out cheerfully and expectantly: "Any Requests?" and the immediate answer was "Yes. F**K OFF!!"

Poor Jock thought he had been cheering us up when really he'd been driving us deeper into despair. Funnily enough, I saw Jock years later in Birmingham with the Salvation Army band - they must have heard him play too because he was only standing at the side of the band collecting the money.

We all did what we could to get through the days which were becoming more torturous as we weakened through lack of nutrition and lack of treatment for our wounds. The only water supply was a lone tap in each barrack building, cold of course, so some lads had got some bits of metal from an old Red Cross powdered milk can and bent it into shape, connected it to the electric lighting supply and would use it as an electrical element to heat water for tea and coffee (when we were lucky enough to have some). These makeshift heating elements or mini-kettles were called "Blowers" because besides being extremely dangerous they would often result in the fuse board blowing and all the lights going out. Another invention born out of our desperation was a little wind-up fan to put a bit of a breeze on cinders from the dying fire to make the heat last just a little longer. We had a wood burner in the middle of the room, but not much to burn. When the nights got particularly bad some blokes would take the wooden slats from under the mattresses and burn those. By spring, the beds became very close to collapsing.

It was well into April before we were released. Rumours had been growing of the allied advance into Germany, and we heard and saw more and more of our planes passing overhead. On the night of the 16th, we were certain our rescue was imminent. Not only because of evidence from the skies outside, but because the number of guards in the camp had drastically diminished over the last few days. All that was left were a handful of the oldest, most unfit men - the minimum of staff needed to keep us held in - the rest had scarpered. There had been a German barracks just down the road from our prison and we would often hear them chanting as they paraded, "March against England!" but now there was silence. That night, I spent some hours on the outer perimeter fence, together with one of the sentries believing our troops might come in the night. He was happy to have my company and shared his fags with me, I suppose he feared what would happen when the British forces arrived and hoped I'd speak up for him.

They came the next day at 11am on April 17th 1945. The sight of British troops outside the wire fence meant our ordeal was over. We saw tanks roll past, some of the relief forces threw white bread, chocolate and cigarettes over the fence and within a few hours the gates were opened and we were freed.

Before we left we had a rummage round the prison office. I remember finding a big book with photos of all the prisoners in it. I flicked through and grabbed my own mugshot, taken when I had arrived and wearing a borrowed Belgian Army Jacket (mine was torn from the bullet I received) and holding up my prison number 117616. I kept that photo with me for a long time and wish I still had it but unfortunately it got mislaid after the war. I seem to think a girlfriend pinched it as a memento of me. If I had it now I'd get it enlarged and framed to show that I survived!

After being released from the prison, my friend Harry managed to acquire a motorcycle left by the Germans. As I was an experienced driver, we used it to follow the tanks into the town.

We found two young German women and a grandmother crying outside the local jewellery shop. It was a family business and the shop had just been looted by some men from one of the allied armies. They had taken everything of value and left the owners in a frightened state. One of the women was called Frau Buhring and although we men were not officially allowed to fraternize with the locals we found them charming. They gave us bread and chocolate and we were made welcome in their home where we had our first bath in six months.

Thirty years later I visited this same shop in Germany and bought my wife a gold necklace.

Harry and I had a run on the motorcycle just for the joy of being free at last. We even went down country lanes not yet liberated. We came across a women's prison that the guards had abandoned. The frail inmates looked bewildered and were all in bad condition from under nourishment, they were close to starvation. We had no idea what nationality they were. It was a shocking sight for us to see female civilians tortured like this and we were beginning to see and comprehend the extent of suffering the war had brought.

We called at a farmhouse to try to get some food - maybe bread and eggs. The poor farmer and his wife looked very scared at our arrival, they saw our uniforms, although grimy and worn still distinctly British, and must have feared for their lives. But we had no quarrel with them or any other Germans. We just wanted to get home.

We did, however break into a German warehouse, just for the fun of it to see what we could find. Inside it was stacked high with crates of perfume and leather wallets. We took some of the stuff as souvenirs. It was wrong, but I guess we felt we deserved something back for what we had suffered over the previous months and after all, the Germans had taken their own souvenirs from us when they confiscated our watches, jewellery and other personal items. Our thefts were a lot less of a crime than some of the things that went on. When our prison camp was liberated, the remaining German guards (most of them had fled) were bundled roughly into a room. I didn't see what happened but can imagine they came out with more than a few bruises. Many of the allies had nothing but contempt for the Germans, not just the soldiers we had been battled against but any German, including women and elderly civilians. Many private houses were looted and occupied and the furniture trashed and the owners forced to work like slaves to please their captors. I saw an old German man trying to sell some cigarettes to the allies, just to earn a few pfennigs to buy food - his cigarettes were grabbed and the poor man was pushed around and humiliated. I felt very uncomfortable when I saw this sort of behaviour. I remember witnessing a similar sort of arrogance from some English lads in uniform back home when I'd been a driver. We often stopped on route and housewives would offer us drinks as refreshment, pleased that they were supporting the troops, the lads would take the drinks and leave without returning the cups and the jug that the woman had kindly brought out. It just seemed unkind and unnecessary to me.

There were a few days left in Germany while the other prison camps were liberated and we were fed and able to shave and wash. We were also deloused with DDT which cured our parasite problem immediately, quite a relief after more than six months of constant itching. We were then sent to Munster airport to return home. We were crowded into the back of a Dakota, all of us eager to get to leave Germany and see our families and friends again. The plane was overloaded and on the first attempt at take-off the back wheel didn't leave the ground. The plane taxied itself back up the runway while we all shuffled around inside, trying to distribute the load and at the next attempt it took off. I remember looking out of the window as we flew over Belgium and seeing the ruins of buildings that had been hit by bombs. It was a dismal sight, but our hearts were warmed by the fact that now the war was over, there would be no more destruction. We touched down at Great Missenden in England on 24th April 1945 and I realised this was the first time in my fifteen flights that I had ever landed in a plane rather than jumping out of it.

At Great Missenden we were extremely relieved to be back on British soil once more. We had all lost much body weight during our time in the German prison and we were skinny, weak, anaemic and bedraggled. People at the airport stopped and stared at the line of thin yellow men leaving the plane. We were taken to a medical centre to be checked over. We were weighed and assessed and all the staff came to look at us, amazed that we had survived.

The utter hardship of my war time experiences still haunts me, but I have the reward of survival. Life went on for me with marriage, children, grandchildren, career, holidays - all the usual stuff, good times and bad times. I still think of Tommy and all the others whose lives were stopped some sixty-five years ago. It all seems so unfair, so unjust and so unnecessary and my heart cries for them.

CHAPTER 8

After the War

The war was over by early May 1945 but we were not
discharged from our regiment straight away. We were given new
uniforms in April on the day of our arrival in England, our old
ones were no more than rags after six months in the prison
wearing them day in and day out. We were also given six weeks
leave with double rations. Rationing of food and some other
items had been in place throughout Britain during the war and
continued on many items for some time afterwards. So with our
extra ration coupons we were able to buy twice as much of these
foods than civilians were able to purchase, if they were available
of course. We felt honoured to be treated so well and certainly
appreciated the contrast to the conditions endured whilst abroad.

My first night out after I returned back to England found me in
more trouble. I went to a local pub, it was 'The George' in
Slough, with some of the other lads and we got drinking. I
hadn't tasted alcohol for well over six months and my body was
currently very underweight and ill-nourished. I was unprepared
for the results. I was drunk after a few sips of beer and somehow
managed to get myself into an argument with a local civilian and
ended up with *his* fist in *my* face. That's all I remember. Next
thing I knew I was back in jail - my fourth prison spell in less
than a year! Luckily things were sorted out quickly this time and
I was released the next day.

I didn't go back home to Croydon to see Dad and Gwen because the house that had been my home as a teenager was now sold, Dad had packed up and moved back to the Cotswolds. What had not occurred to me was that Dad had had no news at all of my whereabouts during my time as a POW. I had been reported missing and that was all. As far as he was concerned I could well be dead. My poor Dad had suffered much grieving in his life and for over six months he believed he had lost his only son too. He'd listened to the Red Cross reports on the radio listing those found, whether dead or injured but my name never came up. The Red Cross were terribly overworked during those years with so many thousands of men killed it was very hard to complete any lists accurately. Three months after I'd gone missing at Arnhem, my Dad had received a letter from the army to say that my pay had been stopped as I was missing. It was too much and he had sold the house in Croydon and moved back nearer to his roots, this time he had found a home in the Forest of Dean at Howle Hill. Fortunately, he still had a little hope for my safe return and had informed the War Office of his whereabouts. I think that the tiny glimmer of hope left in him was inspired by his French pen pal, the friend that he had made during his own time as a prisoner of war in the First World War. They were still writing to each other regularly and in one of the letters received by my dad his friend writes:

".....do not be downhearted, I hope and wish with all my heart that your son had the same fate as you and I had during the last war....".

All Dad could do was wait until war ended and see if I turned up, which thankfully I did.

Cerisiers, C^{ne} de Lapeyrouse (Puy-de-Dôme) 31th January 1945

Dear old Friend,

How happy I was, a few days ago, when receiving your friendly Card, posted more than two months ago! But how sorry I felt when reading that you had not heard from your son since September! Don't be downhearted, dear old friend! I hope and wish with all my heart that he had the same fate as you and I had both during the last war, and that perhaps you know it now. Anyway, I am sure he will come back home safely in the course of the present year.

Kind words to my dad from his French pen-friend

While at Great Missenden I had been told his new address and sent a telegram to let him know I was alive. I was also granted a free travel warrant to go and visit him. Dad hired a taxi and met me at Ross-on-Wye station, and naturally he was overjoyed to see me alive and well with his own eyes - it was such a huge relief for him after all those months of worry. They were living in a lovely house on the side of a hill. Gwen had made a room up for me which looked out across the summery landscape. It was a beautiful view. After six months of being locked in a prison camp surrounded by barbed wire and crowded in amongst dirty, smelly men in ragged clothes, it was a joy to have my own room with clean sheets, the ability to come and go as I pleased, the joy of decent food and on top of this, such magnificent scenery. The house was positioned overlooking forest, fields and farmland. Dad had a mains supply of fresh tap water too, and a flushing loo! I was convinced it was the best place in the world for anyone to live though I'm sure my sentiments were exaggerated by the contrast of what I had just come from.

There was a pub called 'The Crown' within walking distance and I'd walk through the woods to reach it. It stood in a field with real green grass, trees, plants and flowers. I'd often go there for a couple of pints and got to know a few of the locals. I spent a lot of my time helping Dad with his land. He'd retired from the post office now and was making a go at earning some money on a smallholding. He had over an acre and hired a plough and horse to prepare the ground to grow swedes and cabbages to sell. He also had some geese and some sheep. He kept a garden too so there was always something to do. I began to get fit again in no time. It was such a pleasure to be outside in fresh air and if there was no work to be done I would go for long walks in the area.

I was out walking one day when I saw Janet's headmistress from the local school, she said she'd like to speak to me and gave me a lift home. She asked me if I would go into the school to talk to the children about my prisoner-of-war experiences - but I declined. The memories were still too raw and painful.

The six weeks leave seemed to pass extremely quickly. Before long we were ordered up to Newcastle where we spent some time catching up on news, politics and general information of all the things we had missed while in prison. There were lots of military personnel there from different sections of the forces, some had spent many years of the war in prison and had a huge amount of catching up to do. Some had had no everyday news for over four years so needed to know what life in Britain was like now. We were also given lots of information about the new "Beveridge Plan". This was the name given to the newly planned National Health Service.

We were then officially discharged from service - a huge relief to us all. I had originally joined the army with Ray Annets back in 1939 as a way of securing a free summer holiday, nothing more, and since then I had seen horrors I could never have imagined. I had suffered injury and near starvation and seen scores of men die horrible, bloody and agonising deaths. It was more than a relief to be back home safe and with the knowledge that the war had ended there would be no more killings.

Next, at Catterick Barracks, we had medicals and were assessed for pensions - depending on how severely injured we were. Many men had lost limbs or ears or eyes. My only injury was a gunshot wound to my arm. This wound that had seeped and smelt and oozed pus and caused agonizing pain all through the six months of captivity, had now healed up within weeks. The malnutrition had prevented my body from healing itself, but once I was back on a healthy diet it had got rapidly better. Thankfully, I did not need any more operations and I was assessed as 40% disabled at the time for the purposes of my War pension. I got a reasonable amount as a Private, but of course had I have been an Officer I would have been awarded more - doesn't seem fair to me, a disability is unfortunate for any man but I would have thought *more* unfortunate for someone who is likely to have expected to earn a future living from manual work rather than sitting at a desk. I still have a scar and a slightly misshapen joint, but for me there was no real handicap compared to so many others. We were all given a new suit, shirt, tie and shoes and £100 as back pay for our time as prisoners of war. This was a lot of money to receive at once. An average wage for a postman at that time was £3 a week and £3 12s for a bus driver. It was certainly a lot of money for me, and I regret to say that I squandered most of it immediately. I was very irresponsible and I gambled a lot of it away at the dog track. My only defence is that after months of confinement in grim conditions I needed to relax and enjoy myself a bit.

It was now the summer of 1945. Directly after the war, food, jobs and houses were all in short supply - many homes had been destroyed or damaged by bombs. The discharged army personnel were all looking for work at the same time and rationing was still in force on many items. I went back to the Post Office in East Croydon where my Dad had worked, this time as a driver. I rented a room locally. I was now close to being twenty-four years old and keen to get on with the rest of my life.

I looked up some of my mates from the regiment. Bill, who had escaped back to England before my own capture by the Germans, had not however escaped prison. The army had made him serve the remainder of his twenty-eight day sentence that had been cut short when we joined 'Operation Market Garden'. We had a laugh at that, it had seemed unfair to him at the time, but at least he'd had some decent meals in the old stable block at Leicester and been spared our ordeals in Stalag. Our '10th

Battalion' were to meet up regularly for official reunions at Leicester for many years. I attended about half a dozen myself, the last time in 1999.

I visited Harry at his home in Liverpool. He had three sisters and I dated one of them, Cis, taking her to the cinema, to dances and to a formal dinner hosted by the Mayor in honour of servicemen. The relationship with Cis didn't last longer than my time spent in Liverpool, which was six weeks. Harry was a good laugh and fun to be with which was something I needed. I remember one night we found a Church Hall full of people celebrating. They were sailors who had just come back from the far east and it was a private function, but we thought it was a temporary pub, or a dance or something so we went in and up to the bar where Harry ordered two pints, when the bar man said there was no charge Harry said "Make it eight then!" That was not the last I saw of Harry. He came to stay with me when I settled back in Croydon. We stayed in digs together and it was while he was here that he met his wife, Anne. Anne was working in Sainsbury's in George Street where we would take our ration cards and buy meat and other groceries. Anne had been married before but had been sadly widowed in the war, she had a house and she invited Harry and me to lodge there. It was convenient for us all, but when Harry and Anne got married they sold the house and moved away. I lost touch with them for a while, though I'd heard he'd gone to Rhodesia to work in insurance, I didn't see him again until the fifties.

I also contacted a couple of other mates that I'd met during the war - Ken Kirkham and Ray Annets. Ken had been with me at

Arnhem, but when I'd been taken prisoner I had no idea what had happened to him. It turned out that he missed out on the organized evacuation from Oosterbeek but had escaped on his own from Holland with the help of the Dutch Resistance movement. I was glad to know he was safe and well and had avoided capture and got back to England. He'd also appeared in a film about the incidents of 'Operation Market Garden' entitled 'Theirs is the Glory' which was a reconstruction drama/documentary made without actors and using only genuine servicemen and Dutch civilians with experiences of the time. Ken later married one of Harry's sisters, Dot. I saw Ray again too. I'd lost touch with him in the RASC and had last seen him when we were stationed at Feltham together. Ray was now running his own transport company called Annets Transport Co. and he lived in Shirley Avenue in Shirley, Croydon.

In 1946 I was lucky enough to meet a great lady called Joan Cobley. We met at the Locarno Dance Hall in Streatham (later renamed as The Cat's Whiskers). The local dance hall was a popular way of meeting people in those days. Joan was a few years younger than me and originally came from Ipswich though she had spent some of the war years with her Aunt Gerty in Wales. She was now living in Mitcham with a family friend, also called Gerty, and was working in a local hairdresser's shop. As the months passed, I began to see less of the dog track and more of Joan. We often went to Wandsworth for a night out either dancing or to the cinema to see the latest releases - Hitchcock, Clark Gable, Trevor Howard, Vivien Leigh and the likes. I was earning £3 5s as a driver at the Post Office. Beer was about sixpence a pint and a cinema ticket about two shillings so

I could afford a few nights out a week. Joan and I courted for some time sending each other lots of letters to keep in touch as neither of us had a telephone at home. The mail was pretty good in those days, so a letter posted in the afternoon would almost certainly arrive at its destination by the next morning.

Joan and me as a young courting couple

I went to meet her parents a few times in Ipswich, Jim and Gwen Cobley. Joan was an only child, like me. Her mum was a school teacher, her dad had been in the forces in his youth and had various jobs since then. Joan and her family certainly had a sense of humour. When we visited their house I was always a bit put out by its general musty smell and thought things could do with a clean up. I hadn't mentioned this to Jim and Gwen of course but Joan knew. Once when we got there, I was trying my best not to look uncomfortable whilst in the unhygienic kitchen when Joan spotted a bit of old cheese in the larder.

"Colin likes a bit of cheese," she said "and he especially likes it really mature."

Jim handed me the plate with a dried up crust of something that looked like a piece of yellow, crumbling brick, white flakes around the edges and large, sweaty cracks down one side.

"Is that mature enough for you boy?" he said.

I didn't realise they'd set me up and sat there eating the lot pretending to enjoy it, desperate to impress my future in-laws - I had recently proposed to Joan.

Joan and I were married in September 1948 at Croydon Registry Office. I had written to my Aunt Maud (my mum's sister) in Much Marcle as I knew that she had kept Mum's wedding ring and I wanted to give it to Joan. Although Dad hadn't kept in touch with his sister-in-law or her family, I had visited my cousin Gwen during the war years. She was working as a school teacher in Canterbury, I remember her being very afraid whenever there was an air-raid, as many people were, and she would hide under the table in the air-raid shelter. Her mum Maud was kind enough to send the ring to me by post and luckily it fitted Joan perfectly without alteration.

We kept the wedding event small. I wore my de-mob suit and Joan bought herself a new dress. I invited a few of my mates from the Post Office and Joan had a few friends from her work (she was now employed in a salon at Sloane Street, near Harrods) and her landlady, but the only relative was Joan's mother Gwen. We were given a few wedding gifts, the only one of which I remember, because I still have it, being a glass wine decanter - from Lady Clarke - one of Joan's customers. It was also a leaving gift, as when we married, we both quit our jobs. Even with two salaries, it would have been very hard for us to afford a home together that was any more than a rented room and so we had made arrangements to move out of London.

Straight after the ceremony and a few celebratory drinks, Joan and I went by train down to Brighton for a three day honeymoon and then we took another train to Wigpool in the Forest of Dean to begin our married lives together.

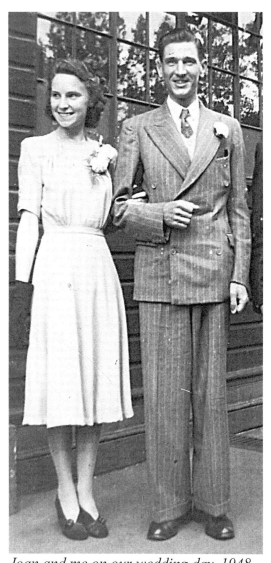

Joan and me on our wedding day, 1948

CHAPTER 9

The Forest of Dean

Dad had recently sold his home at Howle Hill and bought a couple of houses in Wigpool, also in the Forest of Dean, with some land. Before the wedding I had arranged with Dad that Joan and I would move into one of these houses which happened to be right next door to the cottage that he, Gwen and Janet were occupying. Joan and I had never seen the place before but we trusted Dad's judgment that it would be suitable and so we arrived at Wigpool straight from our honeymoon with just a suitcase each with our clothes. I remember the only item in the house was an oil cooker that Dad had set up for us. There was no furniture there yet, we would have to buy it all second hand. We slept on the floor in our clothes until this was arranged, initially blind to any discomfort due to the excitement of our newlywed status.

Now a married man, I began to feel some responsibility as a husband and provider. We needed a place to live that was more than just a room in lodgings so this gift from Dad seemed ideal. He actually gave us the house which was quite small and probably only worth a couple of hundred pounds, but nevertheless a very welcome wedding present. After the war, there was a shortage of housing, especially in the bigger towns like London, as so many buildings had been destroyed in the bombings.

Dad's cottage at Wigpool was called Sunnybank, it's still there now and it came with a fair bit of land that Dad was eager to work on. The house where Joan and I lived was just a few yards away. Actually, it was less of a house and more of a brick shed tacked on to another cottage. There was just one room downstairs to live in and cook in with just the very small stove in the corner and one room upstairs to sleep in. The inside walls were painted in distemper which is a cheap paint, there was no emulsion available at that time and the roof was covered in slate tiles. There was no flush toilet; we used a chemical toilet which had to be emptied daily into a hole in the ground in the back garden. There was no running water; I had to walk to the well with a wooden yolk on my back, the two buckets swinging one on each side. It was a good few hundred yards along a muddy track and through the woods and it was a trip that had to be made at least once a day whatever the weather. I'd fill the buckets from the hole in the ground, about four feet down there was a trickle of water that would pool enough to be able to scoop it up. Then, carefully, I'd attach the buckets back on the yolk and carry them back to the house. The water was clean enough for drinking and cooking but used sparingly as it was such an effort to obtain - for all other water, such as washing ourselves or cleaning the dishes, the clothes or the house we would use rain water which was collected in several rain butts outside. The lack of water wasn't the only discomfort - we had no electricity either. For cooking we had calor gas and for lighting we had candles. We gathered wood from the surrounding area and chopped up fallen trees to use on the open fire, this was our heating when the coal had run out and we couldn't afford more. This was 1948, and we realised that life for us in the Forest of Dean was very much behind the times, but we struggled on knowing that we could not afford any better. We saw Dad and Gwen every day as they lived so close. They had a much bigger detached house and about three acres of land on which they grew swedes and other vegetables, made hay, kept geese and a couple of pigs, a cow for milk and some sheep. Joan helped out with Dad's livestock and she soon learned how to milk a cow and how to salt bacon. We also had a handful of other near neighbours within a minutes walk. We all had to use the same well for water and none of us had electricity.

I soon found employment in Gloucester which was about ten miles away and every morning from Monday to Saturday I would leave for work wearing my Wellington boots and walk one and a half miles along the muddy Forest paths (there were no proper roads) to the nearest station. Sometimes I would make the journey with Jim Durham who lived in another cottage up the track. He came from Liverpool originally and he too worked in Gloucester, his job was at the tax office. We'd walk down the hill to the station, leave our boots with a long line of other men's boots in the station hall, changing into normal shoes, and would catch one of the two trains a day to Gloucester to my job. It was a steam train with just a couple of carriages, taking villagers like me and Jim to work. The trains had two tracks, one each way, except for the tunnel. At the tunnel was just a single track and each time a driver passed through he would take the key hanging on the post (left there by the previous driver) and unlock the gate, drive through and set the key on a post at the other side of the tunnel. If the key wasn't there when a driver approached, it meant a long wait until a train came from the other direction to bring the key through. It usually worked well as the timetable was pretty simple, just two trains in each direction per day, but if the first one each way got held up, then the following one did too. I made another travelling friend on that train, a man who worked in the new 'Television' shop. None of us had ever seen a TV before and were all very interested in hearing about this new technology.

My job was at an ironmonger's named 'Alger & Blackmoor'. The wages were £5 a week, not much, but enough to feed Joan and me. The train would arrive in the town an hour before the shop opened, so I would wait around the corner in Lyon's tea Rooms, with a cup of tea until opening up time.

The ironmonger's shop was run by two brothers, who seemed to totally dislike each other. One of the brothers had a talent for keeping himself drunk and the other had an obvious flair for miserliness. One was a finicky fusspot, the other more of a fastidious faultfinder. They hated each other and they didn't really get on with anyone else either. They were both quite uncouth; I remember a lot of unnecessary public displays of flatulence from them.

The items for sale included all the usual stuff like screws, nails, tools, general building materials and fixings as well as things not available in your usual DIY store today - rabbit snares, rat traps, copper rings for pig's snouts, farm tools, coffin furniture, shrouds and coffin linings, and shot gun cartridges. There was also a blacksmith in the back of the shop who would sharpen knives and shears. All the goods were labelled, not with prices, but with a code. This meant that the actual price could be changed depending on the suspected wealth of individual customers and as many of the items were in short supply after the war and hard to come by, the customers had little choice where to shop. The code was 'DONCASTER'. This word has nine different letters, one for each of the digits from one to nine. So if and item was labelled D it would be 1d, if it was O it would be 2d, N was 3d etc. If it was DD it was 11d, if it was D/D it was 1s 1d and D/N/S would be £1 3s 6d - and so on. Confusing at first and uninterpretable to the customers but easy to follow once you know the system. These price codes, of course, only indicated the minimum price, because if at any time it was assumed that a customer could pay more, then a quickly thought up amount was added to that minimum figure to produce a price to suit each unfortunate and unsuspecting purchaser. The other staff, Mr Humphreys (the manager), Miss Harmer and Mr Palmer (assistants like myself) were encouraged to add on as much as we could whenever we could. Perhaps because the two brothers were so willing to fleece their customers, they held careful guard over the takings. Each time we opened the till, we had to have another staff member verify our actions. Calls such as "Shilling - check!" or "Two and six - check!" were a constant sound. The cunning brothers had a spy hole from the backroom to the shop, and seemed never to miss a thing.

On the spot price increases were not the only way to increase profit margins of the business; the more 'frugal' of the brothers also had an ingenious way of saving a few pennies. There was a WC out the back, for staff, and he would use old rolls of till receipts as toilet paper.

Our employers made us all work hard and if one of them suspected that we were taking too long to serve somebody or getting involved in a bit of conversation with a customer, he would call from the back room "Whoop it to them" meaning "Bung the price up, close the sale and get rid of them and do some work". There was always plenty of tidying and sorting and shelf-filling to be done. The stock arrived at the shop in wooden crates, delivered by rail to Gloucester station and by a railway lorry to the store. These crates had to be emptied and returned as there was a deposit on them which had to be claimed back. It was while I was sorting out these boxes in the store room and moving things around that I got my first tongue-lashing from one of my employers. Unknown to me, the stock room had a hole in the roof. If the brothers hadn't been so mean they probably would have fixed it, but they didn't and when it rained, water would drip onto the floor. Unwittingly, I had placed some stock, and it was expensive stock, under this hole and it had become ruined.

"Hall!" I heard the brother yell, "HALL! You couldn't have placed this stock more precisely under the leak if you'd used a micrometer."

We had a lunch break, one at a time, I usually went across the road to the baker's where they sold dripping cakes which were cheap and filling, though I'm not sure about their nutritional value. I had a few surprise customers too. One was my old school mistress from Broadway, Miss Simmester. I recognized her immediately though I had to tell her who I was not having seen her for some fifteen years since I was about twelve years old. I also served the famous painter and ornithologist of the time, Peter Scott, he was quite a celebrity in his day.

The shop was at 57 Westgate, Gloucester but today it is no longer an ironmonger's store. Presently it is a branch of the Nationwide building society and no trace of what it once was. Next door is a book shop, and on the front step, in mosaic tiles is the word "Winfield". This shop used to be Winfield seed merchants and the mosaic front step is the only familiar thing from my days there sixty years ago.

I suffered the job at Alger and Blackmoor for about a year, before I was able to find a more easy-going employer. The chain store of Timothy Whites had a branch in Gloucester just a few doors away and I applied for a position there. They sold a lot of similar products though their lines were more biased towards household items but they still had a lot of regular ironmonger's ware as well as paints and fertilizers, light bulbs and kitchen ware. It held quite an assortment really. With my recent hard earned retail experience in a similar shop I was accepted.

The branch I worked in was run by Mr Mitchell who was also the organist at Gloucester Cathedral. The shop work wasn't much different to my work at Alger and Blackmore, it was still a crummy job for a crummy wage but it was less pressure, no forced fiddling of the prices and I earned a tiny bit more too. The most important thing to me was that I was able to learn the art of window dressing. I worked hard and was able to style the arrangement of goods in the window to attract customers. I did all the fancy italic writing on the handwritten signs adding a bit of humour here and there, for example, I'd call the chamber pots "Breakfast Cups" or describe the Polyclens (brush cleaner) as "ideal for cleaning parrots". It was the sort of humour that in those days would get people looking, get them interested and get them in the store. The shop was altogether more modern a place than my previous experience at the ironmonger's. It was well lit inside and so more comfortable to work in and there was a crane around the side for lifting stock into the upstairs storerooms which was so much easier than carrying heavy crates up a flight of stairs. I can't say that I enjoyed it there, but things were getting better for me and for Joan with the extra money coming in.

The shop in Westgate is still there, but no longer a Timothy Whites. Last time I visited it was selling jeans, but down the alley to the side are the offices of the local paper, 'The Citizen' which was there when I worked there. It's the paper I used about two years later to place an advert to sell our first house that had been gifted to us by Dad and also to sell the second one we were just about to buy.

We were able to buy this second house as Joan had found a job for herself in the village of Cinderford at the bottom of the hill at the local hairdresser's and after a while we were able to afford to take out a mortgage on another house and two fields in Wigpool. It was bigger than the one up one down we were presently occupying and soon we would need the extra room as Joan was now expecting our first baby.

We'd moved to the Forest of Dean straight after our wedding because we really didn't have any other choices for a home together. We tried to make a go of it, we both worked hard but even in our new house, which was called 'Point Cottage', life didn't really become any easier. The whole way of life there was very tough. Not just the lack of electricity and running water but the fact that no deliveries could be made to the house in winter as lorries were unprepared to make the drive up a muddy track and risk getting stuck. This meant we had to order all our coal for the fire in the summer and store it. When I bought some second hand furniture from an auction sale at Lea Bailey we had to fetch it all ourselves pushing it up back up to our house on handcarts. There was no tarmac or gravel or any sort of constructed road at all. Everywhere was mud. The nearest Doctor was at Mitcheldean, some three miles away down the hill with a steep, muddy climb back up. Joan actually got lost in the woods once trying to find her way home. The nearest pub was too far to walk to for a quick drink, and the nearest shops were about five miles away, which meant a bus ride there and back followed by a tough walk and carrying all our food back up the hill. I often did a bit of shopping in Gloucester after work which meant missing the train and taking the bus which took longer but at least I could bring fresh bread and cheese home with me each day. We got our milk from a farm a mile down the hill and we would buy paraffin for the heater from them and a huge and heavy battery for the radio. Once a week Joan might go to Ross-on-Wye, a town that was good for general shopping, but it was a long bus ride away.

I tried to grow a few vegetables in one of our fields. Every evening after returning from work, I would dig two trenches across the field and put in a couple of rows of potatoes. They were cheap potatoes that had been rejected by the shops as less than perfect and called 'pig-potatoes'. It looked like we would get a bumper crop with all the digging and planting I had done over the weeks - I'd covered about an acre of land and I certainly felt like we deserved it after a lot of hard labour as well as six days a week at work in the store, but what I hadn't counted on were the sheep that roamed around freely all over the hill. It was custom then, and in some places still is, that anyone who owned sheep could let them wander free and graze where they wanted. One evening on returning from Gloucester I came home to an empty field. Some sheep had arrived and must have felt the need for some fresh green leaves and shoots. My young potato shoots were all gone - the sheep had eaten the whole lot and my crop was destroyed. I was heartbroken - my hours and hours of back-breaking work had been for nothing. Dad straight away hedged off the area, but it was too late for that field. I grew a few other vegetables in my little fenced off garden and there were plums to pick everywhere, both Blaisdon Reds and Pershore Yellows, but I'd become disheartened as a would-be farmer. I also tried earning a few shillings by renting out the old brick shed in the corner of one of the fields, but that didn't work out too well either. It was occupied by a lady known as Rhona Meadows (sometimes known as Rhona Durham) the sort of lady who enjoyed visiting the local villages and entertaining men for cash. Quite a friendly lady, who Joan would often chat to at the bus stop, but unfortunately she was not good at paying her bills and when her five shillings a week rent became ridiculously overdue I was forced to get a court order to evict her. She was moved out by the bailiff only to move back in as an unwelcome guest soon after. Once again I had her removed by the court and this time Dad moved one of his cows into the shed - that put a stop to her ideas of squatting. I heard later that she'd opened a pub in Ruredean, though I never visited.

Dad had his own problems with neighbours too. I have to admit he was becoming a bit of a grumpy old man and it must have been hard for anyone to get on with him. Dad managed to fall out with our immediate neighbours, a couple called Mr and Mrs Davies. They had three children and one day Dad caught the children mucking about pulling plums from the trees. I'm not sure if he got things a little out of proportion, after all, plum trees were abundant in the Forest of Dean, but he complained to the parents and harsh words were spoken on both sides. Dad fell out with some other neighbours when he shot their dog - it had been worrying his sheep, and although within the law (the case went to court and Dad won) the neighbours were of course extremely upset over the loss of their pet. Life becomes difficult in such a small community when you only have half a dozen neighbours and you stop speaking to some of them.

The conditions in Wigpool were bad but there were good times too. The view from the hill was wonderful. We could see as far as Ross-on-Wye and also the Brecon Beacons (part of the Black Mountains of Wales). It was very scenic, particularly in the spring with the blossom of plum and apple trees. We also had the arrival of our first baby to look forward to. Joan went into labour one weekend and we called an ambulance, from the neighbours phone, to take her to the maternity hospital. We had to walk to the bottom of the hill for it to pick us up. We travelled to the Sunnyside Maternity Hospital in Pittville Circus Road in Cheltenham and our son was born on Sunday 7th August 1949. We were stuck for names and so picked one out of the Radio Times magazine - Alan. So our new son was named after some radio presenter or technician of the day, I can't remember who, we just liked the name.

Joan stayed at Sunnyside in Cheltenham with our new son for a couple of weeks, as was the general custom in those days and I was able to rent a room in Gloucester for that time so that I could travel to visit her and Alan everyday after work - it would not have been possible to do this and get back to the remote Wigpool.

When baby Alan was a couple of weeks old, we brought him back with us to our home, Point Cottage, though we didn't stay there long. We gradually settled back into a routine and tried hard to make the best of things. As every parent knows, looking after a new baby in the most luxurious surroundings isn't always easy, but Joan certainly did well to care for Alan with no running water, no flush toilet and the nearest shops five miles away. She read countless baby books and information leaflets and took advice from other mothers and grandmothers but the one thing Joan and the baby couldn't agree on was trying to feed to a timetable. Alan was a big boy and wouldn't sleep through the night for many months - he was just too hungry. One night we had to take him to our friend Peggy, who lived about a hundred yards away, and let her look after him just so we could get a good night's sleep!

The new expense of a baby and the loss of Joan's income meant that money was tight. We decided to move back to the shack that belonged to Dad and rent out our own house. Living conditions were less comfortable, but it meant we could save up some money. As the days and weeks and months went on the other hardships that I've already outlined seemed more of a burden than before - the sheep eating our crops, the frequent trips to the well for clean water and the lack of transport all made life in the Forest of Dean not worth continuing with and we decided it would be best for all of us to get back to London. I have to say that Joan coped marvellously with the conditions and rarely complained. I was more used to hardship after spending six months in a prisoner of war camp and after seeing the bloodiness of Arnhem, but Joan had been evacuated to Wales in the war and had lived in comparative comfort all her life so it really was quite a contrast for her. The reason we had come here was lack of money to afford accommodation in London, but it seemed we were going to suffer from lack of money anywhere and at least the humblest of rooms to rent in London would have running water and flushing toilets and so we decided to go back. Despite the magnificent views and the abundance of fresh air, the Forest was really a poor, deprived and scruffy area - not much better than a city slum - except more spread out and surrounded by trees.

My job at Timothy Whites was going well and I had learnt a lot about sales, customer service and window dressing. I must have impressed the firm to some degree as when I applied for a transfer to a London branch it was immediately granted and very soon after I was given a position at the Sutton branch of Timothy Whites.

Joan was just as keen as me to move but we decided I would go to London alone, get settled in the job and search for the best accommodation we could afford before Joan and Alan followed. It was hard for all of us to be apart, I missed Joan and the baby and Joan missed me. For those few months, I would go to the phone box on the corner of Cheam Village each evening and call Peggy, our only telephone owning Wigpool neighbour, where Joan would be waiting ready to receive the call. If we sold Point Cottage we would have enough for a large deposit and with my secure employment I could get a mortgage, and in the mean time, Joan and Alan stayed in the little cottage that Dad had given us. It all worked out very well and in a few months I had found a suitable semi-detached three bedroom property in Wallington. Point Cottage was sold, the land too - it went to the Forestry Commission who I believe still own it. We took about £500 for everything and were able to close the mortgage and use the excess for a deposit on the Wallington house. I travelled back to the Forest where Joan was waiting packed and ready. I hadn't seen little Alan for a while, he was now walking and talking and I remember him saying to me,

"I know you. You're my dad!"

It made me feel that our family had been split apart for too long. We bundled our furniture onto a handcart and wheeled it down the muddy track to the nearest road where the furniture van was waiting and began the drive back to London. Our plight in the

Forest of Dean was over.

Joan and me in Wallington with our two oldest children, Alan and Val

CHAPTER 10

Wallpaper Years

The house in Wallington seemed like a palace compared to our previous home. It cost £1,895 and I had to do a bit of work on it - there had been a burst pipe and a ceiling needed replacing. I also did a re-wire and got new carpets but it was such an improvement on our past that we didn't mind spending some time fixing it up. We now had the much missed clean running water from a tap, a flushing toilet, a bath, electricity, coal fires for heating and besides the home comforts; we had shops to buy food just around the corner. There was also a nursery school, a swimming pool, parks, cinemas, pubs, and all the amenities most of us take for granted within easy walking distance. We felt like we had stepped out of the dark ages into the modern world. We got on well with all the neighbours, of whom there were many more than had been in Wigpool. In 1953 a whole crowd of us gathered in Reg Croton's living room to watch the Queen's Coronation on television. Hardly anyone had a set back then, so these multi-neighbour gatherings went on all over the country on that day. There must have been twenty-five or thirty of us all crammed into his tiny front room for a couple of hours.

I had to work hard to support us all. Money was still a big issue, especially with the mortgage and I applied myself at work, learning all I could at Timothy Whites and was soon given a promotion to store manager and then relief-store manager for other branches. This meant covering for the managers on holiday or off sick. I might do a week here or a couple of weeks there, chopping and changing locations frequently. Back in the fifties, Timothy Whites had many branches all over the country and enough in the London, Kent and Surrey areas to keep me busy. It suited me well as I got to travel a bit and learn more from the other staff. I travelled by train as far as Orpington, Sidcup and Dover. It was funny going back there after my days stationed there in the war. I worked at lots of London branches too - Chelsea and Kensington for examples and I had a few famous customers in some of those branches I visited - the actor Gerald Campion (he played Billy Bunter), the well known Jimmy Edwards (who coincidentally had been one of the aircraft pilots flying to Arnhem with me back in the war) and the Princess Royal (Princess Mary).

We were relatively comfortable but we weren't well off at all, paying the bills was still a struggle. At one point, we even had to rent out the upstairs floor of the house. Joan, Alan and myself slept downstairs and the bedrooms upstairs were let out to a nice young couple called Tom and Sheila. We added a little kitchen of sorts with a cooker, a sink and cupboard so that the rooms would be more independent but we all had to share the bathroom. The rent money helped somewhat with our bills but we were still counting every penny and every shilling that came in and went out. Joan and I had a little tin money box, divided inside into several sections with slots in the lid for each one. We used this to save up towards bills such as electricity, rates, coal etc, putting in a few coins each day. It worked well and helped us keep money aside for when it was needed. We felt that we would be able to cope when the bills came, but we hadn't counted on losing the lot in one go. Back in the fifties, it was common not to lock windows and doors all the time. We knew all the neighbours and we trusted our lodgers. One night, in the hot summer, we were burgled, the thief entering through the open patio door downstairs while we slept. He (or she) took the tin box and we were devastated to have all our savings stolen. It was a terrible set back. I was working all the hours I could to provide for my family, and it was taken in an instant. But I suppose it made me want to improve on our situation all the more. I had certainly matured from my Army days when I would shirk any work at the first opportunity. To make up for the stolen money, I took on an extra job in a pub in the evenings. I'd leave Timothy Whites at 6pm and get to the Cricketer's pub at Carshalton for 7pm and then work until closing time at 11pm. It was a period in my life when I was exhausted for most of the time, but I had to keep going to pay the mortgage and look after my family, which was expanding. The pub burnt down a while ago, but I still remember the agony of sustaining two jobs with what seemed like never a moment off.

Our daughter Valerie was born soon after we were settled in Wallington. Her name was also picked from the Radio Times, we chose it after seeing the actress Valerie Hobson listed. With our growing family, it was not too long before I decided that I definitely needed to increase our income and decrease my working hours. I was desperate to give up the pub job and make do with just a day job, but it needed to be better paid for us not to have to struggle with bills. My career at Timothy Whites was never going to progress further than it had and so I set about improving my prospects by applying for another position at another company. I was interviewed and accepted by

'Mourton's' of Croydon. They were a wholesaler of paints and decorating supplies and they had a few retail shops too. Not only was I given a better wage than the £6 10s I had earned at Timothy Whites, but I had the use of a company car as well. I was allowed to use the car for myself at weekends too and it was the only car in our road. Imagine how grand I felt after my terror in the German prison camp and my financial hardships of the last few years, to now be the only person in the whole street with a motor vehicle! The job at Mourton's was the end of our financial insecurities and we never had to struggle again. We weren't rolling in cash but my wages were adequate for a decent life. We had a home, we had home comforts of heating, lighting and water and we had food in the cupboards and anyone who has had to struggle or live day to day to see food on their plate will understand the relief that comes with having a good, steady income.

During the fifties, Joan and I had one more child - a second son who we named Derek (again picked from the Radio times though I don't remember which actor it was). The lodgers had left by now, so the house was big enough for us all. The rental income had been very much needed in the first couple of years, but now with my new job, the mortgage and money for other expenses were no longer so hard to find. We even had a little money to spare for a few luxuries. One of the things we bought was our first own television set. They we just becoming available in the shops at affordable prices and they really were novelty items at the time. Black and white of course, and at first only the one channel - the BBC, but later followed by ITV and BBC2. I remember the thrill we all felt at watching our first TV programme on our own personal set. It was a farming show from Badminton in Gloucestershire. I expect it would seem very boring by today's standards, but extremely exciting at the time and we certainly felt well off to own a piece of such modern technology. The BBC did not run programmes for twenty four hours continuously, like today. Back then it always closed down in the late evening to a broadcast of the National Anthem - though I don't suppose we were the only family to switch off as the opening bars sounded rather than stand to attention.

Another piece of wonderful technology we had was a teas-made. They have gone in and out of fashion over the years but in the fifties we felt very special to be able to be woken with a fresh cup of tea waiting by the bedside ready to be drunk. I never lost interest in the novelty either, we used it for years and years until it finally packed up.

We also bought a dog. It was a golden Labrador and we called him Shandy. He was a beautiful puppy that was adored by all of us. Poor Shandy was only six months old when he became ill, diagnosed with yellow jaundice which he had caught from some water in the park that was contaminated by rat's urine and sadly he had to be put down. It was a terrible thing, the whole family were devastated and I couldn't face owning another dog again. I've only ever had cats since then.

Of course, I still had to work hard, and I did. I can't say that work was my life - my family and my friends were always more important. Joan and I would socialise at the local clubs for a drink or two and I also played snooker. We often went to the horse races at Sandown, Epsom and Kempton Park, sometimes we'd have a small flutter, sometimes we'd just watch. More importantly, I always made sure we had a good family holiday. Besides lots of Sunday excursions down to Shoreham or Selsey for a picnic, we often went for a week to holiday camps on the south coast such as Maddison's at Littlestone near Dungeness, or a similar place at Bracklesham Bay. Places like that would all be very dated now - meals were served in barrack like buildings on long tables, like school dinners and there were even knobbly knees competitions - all the usual "Hi-de-hi" stuff, but the children loved it and we did too. With the company car, it would only take an hour or so to get down to the coast (the roads were very empty in those days!) and we'd enjoy a week by the beach with plenty of fresh air.

Val, Derek, me and Joan at a holiday camp

I worked hard in those years and really made an effort at my job at Mourton's. I learnt a lot about business and was able to advise my father-in-law, Joan's dad - Jim Cobley, on a few issues. Although originally from Wales, he had been living in Ipswich throughout the war. I think he had got a job at a pumping station to avoid being called up (there were certain occupations that were deemed necessary during war time). He'd been a regular soldier in the Royal Engineers previously and had no desire to face combat again. Now, in the fifties, he had moved to London with his wife, Joan's mum - Gwen. They had a flat in Tooting and we visited them often. He absolutely hated that I smoked, and I always felt uncomfortable going there to have him moan about this issue, though I never smoked in his house only outside. Joan didn't mind though and despite the fact that she didn't smoke herself, when I was driving she would often light up my pipe for me, puffing away till it caught and then hand it over to me at the wheel. Jim had had various jobs since the war, he did a bit of clock and watch repair, he'd been involved with a company that made metal staircases, he'd worked on a farm but now he wanted to run a shop, so I was able to help him out.

My experience in retail was in decorating materials so he bought some premises in Golders Green and opened up a paint and wallpaper shop which he called "Walltone Ltd". Dealing with customers was a new experience for him. I remember him saying, "In the war we used to keep pigs and I learned to get on with them, I suppose it will be the same with this lot." He travelled from Tooting to Brent every day on the Northern line of the underground. Each Sunday I would go up there too to dress the windows and do the books. He kept the business for about eighteen months, then sold it on for a good profit and was able to buy his first ever car - a Standard 8. I think perhaps, my help endeared me to him a little more than previously.

At the start of the sixties, my mate Alf and I decided that we could also do as well on our own and so decided to go into business together to earn a bit on the side. Alf was the uncle of the owners of Mourton's, he had his own business - an electrical shop. I'd met him when one of his nephews had sent him along to me to gain some experience of running a shop. We'd become quite friendly and thought we could do well from our pooled knowledge and contacts in the trade. We searched out a warehouse to rent in Barnes to keep our stock which of course we would source from the same suppliers as Mourton's and were about to go ahead when the boss found out. I don't think he was too happy that we were ready to start up in competition with him and he sacked me. It wasn't just that, I'd been working at one of their branches in Hamsey Green at the time. It was a new shop that I'd been fitting out and training up the new staff. I took some long lunch hours during that period, because I wanted to go home for lunch like I always did when I worked closer to home, and with the travelling I was sometimes away for three hours. I must have thought I could get away with it but unfortunately for me the bosses phoned up one afternoon and I wasn't there and the truth came out. I lost my salary of £12 a week, my commissions and my company car with my dismissal but by then I had saved enough to purchase my own vehicle. I bought a Vauxhall Victor. With my firing had come a large lump sum as redundancy money. I have to say that even though my employers had been less than happy with me, they were still very generous with their pay-off.

I was out of work for a while, but I had learnt enough about business by then to feel confident about going self-employed and in 1961 I had enough experience and money to buy my own business, I put my plans of a rival company to Mourton's on hold and instead I bought a newsagents shop in New Malden. The shop came with a large flat above and small garden out the back and so we sold the house in Wallington and all moved in to the flat. Two adults, three children and a cat called Lizzie (later we had three tortoises - Barney, Fred and Bam-Bam). Now I was my own boss and I liked it. Living over a newsagent was probably quite tempting for the children, with all those sweets around, but I didn't notice too much of the confectionery stock disappear - perhaps they were more into the fags by then! I did, however suffer theft of another type. The newsagent was on the route to the local station for a lot of people, a line that went to London - so lots of commuters - and I would leave a pile of newspapers outside on a table with a box for them to put the money in so they didn't have the inconvenience of coming in and queuing just for a paper. It worked well - most people are honest, but occasionally, the box of money would be pilfered. It was only loose change really, but still a theft. One morning I kept watch, behind the counter inside, out of sight from the street. I kept watch for what seemed hours before there was any action. I suppose I shouldn't have told my neighbour, Ross, my plans, because he came creeping, rather conspicuously, and made to take the box. He was only fooling around of course, knowing how bored I must be getting while watching all morning and nothing happening. The real thief was eventually caught some weeks later, apparently he'd done the same thing to a couple of other newsagents along the High Street.

Another time, we nearly adopted a cat. He would come and sit on the newspaper table outside, many people would come up to him exclaiming "Oh, what a lovely cat!" and be ready to stroke him, but he'd reply with a "Hssssssssss!!!" and lash out his claws. He was a stray and a bit wild, but just liked to sit on the table enjoying the sun. He didn't officially belong to us so I won't take the blame.

It wasn't long before the time seemed right to expand my business from just owning one newsagent and so I teamed up with my friend Alf again and together we bought another shop in New Malden High Street, opposite Tudor Williams, in which we sold mainly wallpaper. Wallpaper shops are not very common today, but in the early sixties, fifteen years after the devastation of World War II, wallpaper shops were booming. There were more and more people who were now buying their own homes rather than renting them and they were taking more pride in the homes that they had invested in and so wanted to decorate. In an incredibly short space of time, in business terms, we were able to buy the shop next door to the first one so that we now had a double store in New Malden and shortly after that we were able to buy three more shops. I had to sell the newsagents to raise some of the money, but was happy to do this as the profits on greetings cards and ice-creams were peanuts compared to paint and wallpaper.

The new premises were in Clapham Junction, Stoneleigh

Broadway and Tolworth. We called them all "Elite Wallpapers" and they all did exceptionally well. Saturday's were our busiest days, sometimes it was chock-a-block in the shop and hard to even turn round! I did all the sign-writing and window displays which I was very good at by now. I also fitted out the new shops with shelves and counters which I made myself and managed all the repairs as well as doing all the book-keeping and serving customers. We had a machine for trimming the wallpaper rolls - they would come with a white border on each side and so the edges had to be taken off before it could be taken home by the customer. The roll was threaded through and trimmed then re-wound at the other side - you had to be careful to match the pattern of the paper up to the next roll so that when it was hung it would be hard to see the join. We sold paint too and all the sundries - brushes, cleaners, fillers and the like.

With our past joint experience in the trade, Alf and I were able to source our stock at good prices. I had a little Morris traveller van to pick up stock and deliver to customers. We got a lot of our stock from Mourton's wholesale department - they were still happy to trade with me thankfully. We used other suppliers too - one time I remember buying a whole load of rolls of wallpaper from a warehouse in Croydon. They'd had a burst pipe on the premises and a lot of it was damaged, I suppose after their insurance was settled, they sold off everything without even bothering to sort through it. A lot of it was OK and for months afterwards our house had rolls and rolls of wallpaper stacked up in every available space - there was just too much to put in the shops. Hundreds of them! We bought them for four shillings a roll and made a very good profit. Even the damp stuff was usable - it was good enough for damp walls!

Me trimming the wallpaper

Compared to any job I might have been in such as postman or shop assistant, I was now running four little gold mines. Inflation was high, 27% at one point, and I always said, I could have closed those shops for a year and made such a huge return on the stock when I re-opened them that I would still be way into profits. I didn't close any of them, I worked hard and Joan helped too. For a while she ran the store in Tolworth while I minded the one in Stoneleigh and Alf looked after the Clapham branch and we employed a manager for the other one. Another example of the crazy inflation of the time was when Joan persuaded me that she needed her own car. She was actually quite crafty in her approach. While running the Tolworth store, Joan and the staff girls would deliberately make a point of asking (persuading?) customers if they would like their wallpaper purchases delivered. She'd offer delivery to anywhere - Chessington, Epsom, Surbiton - I'm sure we offered more deliveries than Bentalls (a big department store in nearby Kingston upon Thames). With so much emphasis on the delivery option she had a lot of takers and soon I didn't have time to do them all myself and so Joan 'volunteered' to do it herself, providing of course that she had the necessary transport. We bought a lovely red mini car for her and with a good pedigree too, from the Duke of Northumberland at Syon Park, so very posh. The example of inflation comes in when we sold the car a few years later and got the same price as we paid for it, £500, despite the obvious usage and deterioration - something that would not happen now with what was then a very run-of-the mill, low end of the range and ordinary car.

Alan, who had not been doing very well at school (Elmwood

Road in Wallington), now changed to Beverley Boys school and did much better and Val started at a school in Blagdon Road, New Malden. It seemed my life was picking up all the time. We even had our first holiday abroad, to Italy, in 1962. It was just Joan and Derek and myself. The holiday cost us thirty-nine guineas for ten days - not bad for Italy! Alan and Val were at school and it was too difficult to take them too. They stayed at home and were looked after by one of my shop ladies. She was actually my store detective. Even then, there were plenty of thefts from shops and without today's CCTV it was up to a human eye to catch them in the act. Us shopkeepers in the parade kept an eye open for one another and always kept each other informed of suspicious characters. We had a list of known regular shoplifters which included what you would imagine to be respectable people including a nurse and a teacher. One time in Stoneleigh I popped next door to the Co-op to get some teabags and milk. I knew the manageress quite well so I thought I'd have a laugh one quiet afternoon and casually walked into the store and started, very obviously, cramming groceries into the inside pockets of my coat. As she walked towards me I said "You can't touch me 'til I leave the store!". Luckily she saw the funny side as she chased me out.

It wasn't just the customers who were likely to thieve. I had to sack a few staff for stealing too. One of my employees thought she'd take advantage of handling cash. It was in the Tolworth branch that Joan was looking after. One of the assistants was buying all sorts of stuff that I was sure my wages to her didn't cover, including a car. I was certain she was fiddling me somehow, even though the till was rarely short, but I had to catch her in the act. I filled the place of another staff member who had gone on holiday for a week but with my obvious presence nothing happened. So I got a friend, Ann Bullen, to pose as a customer while I stayed out of sight and sure enough, when Ann went to pay for her goods with the correct money (about £3 I believe) the thieving assistant did not ring it up on the till, she slipped the cash straight into her pocket. Of course, I had to fire her on the spot. There were tears, but no denials - she'd been caught red-handed.

Eventually I split with my business partner, Alf as I felt I was doing more than my share of the work, and we sold the Clapham store and divided the others. He had the New Malden two and I had the Tolworth and Stoneleigh two. By now, my family and I had all moved house again. When we sold the newsagents we had to move out of the flat and so I'd bought a three bedroom semi in New Malden. We lived there for several years - maybe fifteen or so. The children grew up there. When Alan was old enough he got himself a paper round, even battling through the heavy snows of the 1962 to 1963 winter. The drifts were up to his waist and he had to climb over gates and fences to get the papers delivered, but he did them all and I was very proud.

Dad had by now moved again, he had left the Forest of Dean about a year after us and bought a little house with a garden. Tending the fields and the livestock had become too much for him, he was ready to retire fully. He now lived in Hucclecote, near the War Memorial at Green Lane. We saw him now and again but he sadly didn't have many years left. He became ill and suffered a heart attack. He was in hospital for a while and

Alan and I visited, sleeping in my work van over night. Soon after we left, he was discharged and told to take things easy for a while, but my Dad loved the outdoors too much and he'd never been one to sit still for too long. A short while later when the local doctor visited him for a check up, Dad was out in his garden digging a ditch for some project he had in mind. Dad had another heart attack soon after and this time didn't survive. He was well into his seventies when he died. The funeral was attended by Joan and me as well as Gwen and Janet and some of Dad's friends. Gwen remained at Hucclecote only for a short time afterwards and then went to live with Janet, who was now married and living in Cardiff.

Me in one of my paint and wallpaper shops

I stayed in the wallpaper business until the mid seventies. By then, the larger out of town supermarkets and DIY stores were growing and I could see that High Street shopping was declining and the smaller parades like at Stoneleigh and Tolworth were getting less and less popular. The business that I owned had had its peak. I decided to get out while ahead. My children had all grown up and left home by then, Alan was working in Holland, Derek in Australia and Val was about to move to a flat in Tolworth and then later to Spain and so in 1976 I sold the last shop - funnily enough the buyer was Mourton's who I had used to work for. I was fifty-four, but not quite ready to retire - it wouldn't be long before Joan and I decided to start a completely new venture.

CHAPTER 11

Back to Broadway

With the business sold, we had a tidy sum in the bank and plenty of free time. I've never felt comfortable doing nothing, like my dad I suppose, and so I took a part time job. The work involved picking up and delivering vehicles for a car dealership. I'd always done lots of driving so was at ease on the roads and thought it would be quite pleasant work. Some journeys were short such as taking a Jaguar from Collingdale to British Aerospace at Brooklands, but others were longer like from Leeds to Bournemouth. I'd sometimes have to get a train home and Joan would pick me up from the station. At first, I was content as I liked driving a variety of new and sometimes quite flashy cars. The shorter journeys were easy, but soon the longer ones became a drag. One day I had to take a van from Morden, South London to Durham, then pick up another one there and bring it back to Morden. It's a round trip of about 600 miles and it took me all day. My backside was certainly aching from sitting still so long that day. I earned £9 for the eleven or twelve hours that it took me, which seemed just about worth it until I returned home, completely shattered for less than a tenner, to find that Joan had been out shopping in my absence and bought herself a new frying pan which, co-incidentally, cost exactly £9. I felt I'd spent an eternity on the roads just for a frying pan. Suddenly the job seemed pointless and I jacked it in soon after.

I still wasn't quite ready for full time retirement. I'd always fancied the idea of returning to the place where I'd grown up to spend my final years. I expect many people dream of returning to their roots, particularly if they have fond memories of their early years as I had. Throughout the years, Joan and I had taken a few weekends away to Broadway. It was then, and still is, a picturesque village and attracts many tourists. As I was keen to start a new business we thought that running a small guest house in the village would be ideal and so Joan and I began to house hunt.

We must have made six or seven trips in all and each time we searched out a property that we could buy not just to live in ourselves, but one where we could rent out some of the rooms as a Bed and Breakfast establishment. Eventually we found a suitable house at the end of the village. It was a thirties built semi-detached house with five bedrooms - one for us, three for paying guests and a spare. It cost us £21,000 which seemed a considerable sum at the time compared to the £500 my Dad had sold our previous Broadway home for, but that was inflation, and today, no doubt it would have increased much more and cost well into the hundreds of thousands of pounds.

The house needed a bit of work which I was able to do myself once we had moved in. It needed re-wiring, a central heating system had to be installed and there was some paintwork to touch up and new carpets to lay, but none of that took long. We did a makeover inside, buying new beds and a few other bits and bobs and tidied up the garden. Then I made a new sign to name our business, we called it "Wavertrees", and we were ready to take our first customers.

We always made sure the bed sheets were clean and of good quality and that we gave a decent breakfast in the morning. They were the two things we had noticed were often very poor when we had visited Broadway ourselves as paying guests over the recent months. Many of the rival B&Bs seemed to believe that nylon sheets were acceptable, and for breakfast it was common to receive, rock hard tomatoes, see-through bacon and second hand toast that previous diners had leftover. Joan and I thought we could do better and always gave our guests a complimentary tray of tea and biscuits on arrival and in the morning we made sure that we served fresh grapefruit, fruit juice, a full cooked breakfast of bacon, sausage and eggs followed by fresh toast and tea - and all of it decent quality. We both took great pride in offering a high standard and a value for money overnight stay for our guests and we were fully booked all through the tourist season. We even had guests return for a second or third stay as they had found us so good.

I don't remember ever being short of guests - they came not just from the UK but from America and Australia too, though to be honest even our rivals with their sub-standard bedding and used toast did well - it's just a very touristy area!

It was easy money. It seemed we had found another little goldmine. We would get up at seven and prepare the breakfasts, then clean the room, change the sheets, wash up and be out by 10am after sticking the 'No Vacancies' sign in the window so as not to be disturbed until later. We might take a trip to the shops or the Mac Market cash and carry in nearby Evesham for more supplies, then stop at the pub on the way home. We'd take down that sign sometime late afternoon or evening and could be confident we would still have all three rooms filled each night.

Perhaps it was too easy, because before too long we had found a nice pub on the way home from Evesham. It was called the Cider Mill (though I think it has changed hands since our days there in the mid '70s). We called in one day by chance on the way home and found it to be cosy and welcoming. We met a friendly bunch of regulars who we soon became chummy with and before too long we were there every day, drinking, chatting and wasting away the hours. We'd often drink in the evening too - either with our guests (we frequently accompanied guests to the local pubs for a drink) or on our own, or with our local friends. Soon we were both drinking far too much - it just seemed so effortless to slip into a pub two or three times a day with money to spend and not much else to do.

We had mostly good neighbours too. As an old Broadway boy I was welcomed easily into the village and Joan as my wife was accepted too. I'd heard that it could be difficult for outsiders to make a home there but I had the advantage of already knowing a few people. Anne Jacques was a good friend to us, she lived two doors away and ran her own B&B. I remember her as a charming lady whose husband I had known when I was a boy, though he was some ten years older than me. We'd go to her house for coffee or she would come to ours and sometimes we'd shop together. I also met up with a few other people that I had known from my childhood, in particular, Charles Ingles, my old schoolmate. He'd lived in Broadway all his life. I saw a lot of him, it was great to reunite with a friend from my childhood.

Sadly, he passed away a few years ago. He was buried in the graveyard of the church where I was a choir boy all those years ago, a lot of my old mates are and I always stop and pay my respects when I visit the area now.

Even in the winter, we weren't short of guests. There was a prison nearby at Longlarton and we often had visitors to the inmates spend a night with us. We had a couple of long stay guests too - I remember a Mr Burns, meteorologist from Surrey, who wrote 'adult' books in his spare time and would leave pages of his manuscripts in the room which I couldn't help glancing at when vacuuming. We inherited him from a neighbouring guesthouse when they sold up. We also had a late call at 11pm one winter. It was the members of a travelling pop group from Liverpool. They were called 'Lafayette' and were to us just teenagers, and long haired at that, but they were extremely well behaved and courteous. Funnily, we had a lot of visitors from Liverpool - apparently because the name of our house, Wavertrees, was almost the same name as a suburb there and they chose us because of that connection.

For the time we were there, we kept a guest book for visitors to write remarks on their stay. I still have the book and am pleased with all the flattering comments that we received. In fact, the whole time that we were there we only had one less than positive comment and that was from a lady who felt it necessary to moan that we had knocked up our prices since her first visit a year earlier. Most of it reads, "...excellent....first class....couldn't be better....shall come again..." and I am very proud.

We often had non-paying guests too. Alan visited a few times, as did Val and her boyfriend. One time when Val stayed she helped out by running the place for us while Joan and I had a little break. We didn't go anywhere glamorous, just back to Surrey to visit friends. We stayed in a guest house in Tolworth for a week and of course couldn't help comparing the service to our establishment and were pleased to find that this one was not as good as ours! Alan sent some Australian friends from Holland over to visit us in Broadway too. They stayed with us in winter and saw their first ever snow!

Joan and me happy together

We stayed in Broadway for less than two years. The business was remarkably successful, but the money was not enough to keep us there. In the winter, there is very little to do except go to the pub and we were doing too much of that already. Life can be very slow in the country, I remember several times driving back from Evesham we would be held up on the road by a herd of cows. The woman urging them on was anything but urgent in her approach and would half-heartedly coax them along, calling each by name as she did so, "Come along Daisy....keep going Clover....move up now Buttercup....". That day as we sat in the car waiting to pass, I remarked how great it was that she knew all her cows by name, to which Joan impatiently replied, "I've sat here so long, *I* know all her bloody cows by name."

Besides having not much to do, we had a problem with one neighbour or not so much the neighbour but their dogs. They had three Dalmatians which we had been unaware of when we bought the house, but we soon noticed them when we moved in because they would not stop barking. The tiniest thing would set them off. If I opened the back door, if I put something in the dustbin, if they saw a cat, sniffed a bird or even if the weather changed it seemed and we were disturbed every few minutes by barking, yelping and howling never knowing when it would stop and when it did, always on edge never knowing when it would start again. It's a noise that I have never been able to tolerate for long periods and together with our growing worry over the fact that we seemed to be drinking our lives away, we decided that Broadway and Bed and Breakfasts were not for us.

I made a few trips to the South West London area and had soon found a home for us to buy. Whilst looking I found a lovely place in Kingston Hill which I did consider but on seeing how close it was to Richmond Park I decided against it assuming there was bound to be one or more neighbours with dogs and I just could not face that prospect. The property that we eventually chose was a flat in a brand new block at Sutton in Surrey and it cost us £18,500. And so by 1979 we had sold the B&B (we sold the house to the son of our friend Anne Jacques and he ran it for a while though since then it has changed hands again). We'd spent just a couple of years there and I felt more than a bit of regret that things hadn't worked out as planned. I had spent a lot of time in my younger days believing that Broadway would provide a happy retirement for me and Joan and we would live out our last years there together. It had always been something to look forward to but when it became reality the dream somehow lost its appeal. Our next move to Sutton would provide me with the place that was to be my home for the next twenty-five years - longer than I have lived anywhere else.

CHAPTER 12

Retirement, Reunions and Re-tracing my Past

The flat in Sutton was situated close to the shops and close to
the station, we had nice neighbours and no barking dogs. We
were very comfortable there, and financially sound too so
neither of us needed to work. I was approaching sixty and Joan a
few years behind, but neither of us enjoyed an idle life and so
for a while we both got part time jobs. Joan worked at Marks
and Spencer for a short time and then on the Esteé Lauder
beauty counter at Alders in Sutton, but after running our own
business she couldn't get used to the discipline of being an
employee and so eventually gave up work before official
retirement age. I tried my hand at a few jobs too. First I tried
mini-cabbing. I'd always liked driving and thought this would
give me a bit of variety compared to a shop or office job. I stuck
it for a couple of months. The work actually became intolerable.
I had dogs being sick in the car, humans being sick in the car
and I was kept waiting for hours once while a woman searched
for her cat so I could drive them to the vet - you'd think she
would be ready *before* she called for a cab. The traffic was
appalling, especially on the airport runs - both Gatwick and
Heathrow - and it seemed just at clocking off time of 5pm I
would always get a call to the West End and find myself stuck in
more jams for another couple of hours. I remember driving
blokes to the dole office for them to sign on, wait for them and
then take them down the pub. I could see that the unemployed
were having an easier life than me. Besides this, I was using my
own car and the constant use was wearing it out, and my

insurance was bumped up because of the change of use. The effort and stress certainly wasn't worth the money for me and so I quit.

Another job I tried was in the pharmacy of Banstead Mental hospital. The hospital was comprised of about ten old and grand Victorian buildings and is now Downview prison. I would distribute non-prescription sundries such as bandages, scissors and rubber gloves to the staff on the wards. It was fairly monotonous but kept me busy. I left that job after about six months to work for the civil service, at the mail room of the DHSS. Part of the job involved passing on letters to the fraud department. These were usually anonymous tip-offs from members of the public concerning neighbours or people they knew who were falsely claiming state benefits, especially unemployment benefit when they had a job. There were sack loads of it. Eventually a lot of the historic confidential paperwork had to be burnt and we'd tip loads into a furnace. I often delivered folders of cases being investigated to other branches. I remember one case where someone was investigated because paint spots had been seen on their glasses which meant they were possibly decorating when they shouldn't have been able to afford it. Another time, a woman who worked at the Labour Exchange reported a bloke who had just signed on and later found him to be her driver when she called a cab. There were ten of us working in the mail room, all close to retirement having had previous careers - a fireman, a postal worker, shopkeepers and similar. It was a great crowd and we had a few laughs, I was quite settled in that job and remained there for about eighteen months. I would have stayed longer, probably until I was sixty-five - however, I was given the chance of early retirement with a full pension at just sixty. It was a new scheme just brought in by the government at the time to help ease unemployment figures. If you gave up your job five years early, you were rewarded - seemed good to me!

Now that I was sixty, and no longer working, I had a lot of spare time on my hands and needed to fill it. One of the things I liked doing was going up to London on the train. It was just a few stops away from Sutton station and so quick and easy to get to. Often I was happy just to walk around and explore places like Smithfield Market, St Bart's Church, Knightsbridge and Harrods, Covent Garden and the London Parks, marvelling at the buildings, statues and monuments. Sometimes, for a bit of variety, I would go to the public gallery at the Old Bailey to watch cases being tried. I'd take a sandwich and a couple of pork pies, a flask of tea and could spend the whole day up there. I got to witness some famous trials including the Brinks Matt trial and also the case involving the MP John Stonehouse who had faked his own suicide and fled to Australia, as well as the Sonia Sutcliffe versus Private Eye hearing. It was always interesting, better than the theatre I would say. There were twenty courts there and over the years I got to know which courts were the best to go to, I got to recognise barristers and judges and if it was a murder case I could always spot whether they would be found guilty or not a long time before the verdict was announced. Sometimes Joan came with me and we'd really make a day of it. I have to say those early years of retirement in the 1980s were very good for me. We had so much time to ourselves with no commitments of work, children or money to earn. We were both fit enough to get out and about either by car, public transport of by foot and we were able to fully relax for the first time. We both loved walks in the country too and days at the races, enjoyed all the more for not having a timetable. We didn't just stick to the local race courses of Epsom and Sandown, we went as far as Lingfield, Goodwood, Bath, Newbury and Wolverhampton.

We both enjoyed retirement

Joan and I had wonderful times together, especially during the retirement years when we had more time to ourselves. I think our joint sense of humour was one of the things that kept our marriage secure for so long. For example, when I tried to grow some mushrooms indoors from a kit, Joan sneaked open the airing cupboard door where I was keeping them, the same night they were planted, and put a giant mushroom from the greengrocer some six inches diameter in the box for a laugh. I certainly got a surprise the next morning when I checked on them and thought I must have bought some super fast growing variety! I got my own back soon enough when Joan's friend came round to do her hair and I set up a eighteen inch loo brush in a jar with a tube of toothpaste by the bathroom basin and made out that was what she used to brush her teeth. We were always pulling little jokes like that on each other, and always up for a laugh.

During our retirement years, we visited our son Derek in Australia who by now was married with two children - Joanne and Kevin. Derek had gone to Australia as a teenager, travelling all the way by road and sea - across Europe and Asia. He'd visited us in England a couple of times but it was a great adventure to travel across the world to see him and his wife and our grandchildren. They live in a bungalow at Cairns, we stayed for three weeks and had a wonderful time. It was April and hotter than any summer in England. We also visited our daughter Val, who by now had moved to Spain and had two children of her own - Meghan and Alex. She later returned and lived at Tolworth which is fairly close to Sutton so we were able to visit more often. Alan, our oldest child, had returned from Holland and was now married and settled in New Malden, later moving to Epsom which was close to us too.

We also took many holidays during those years. Sometimes we went abroad, all over Europe and the Mediterranean and sometimes even further afield. One trip was to Sierra Leone, a poorer part of Africa in those days, and a place that had seen few tourists before us. We came to this conclusion whilst trying to sunbathe on a beach and finding a group of vultures circling above us assuming we were dead meat - they obviously hadn't experienced idle Westerner's soaking up the sun before. Sometimes we just took a short break in this country, we even went back to Broadway a few times, staying at the Cider Guest House.

I also took a few recreational evening classes including London History, which I really enjoyed and tied it in with our walks round London. I did French Polishing, which wasn't so much fun and I have never used again since and I did Bird Watching which I did use - on our many country walks. Another hobby I pursued for a while was treasure hunting. I bought myself a metal detector for £60 from a shop in Twickenham and would take it on walks, to the parks, the beach or the countryside and spend a few hours walking up and down scanning for items. I actually found quite a lot of stuff - loads of old coins, some of them Elizabethan, gold rings and lots of present day coins. I often went detecting with a friend of mine, Roy, and we would often attract a crowd of kids around us watching to see what we found. I would get a bit self-conscious if all we found was bottle tops and ring pulls but very proud when we dug up something of historical interest or of value. I remember Richmond Park was a good place to find loose change that had fallen from the pockets of courting couples who had been rolling about in the long grass

- at least it was until we got caught by the Park Ranger and told to stop. Another time Roy took me over to West Drayton in Middlesex, somewhere near where he had grown up. I didn't know the area and we were driving round and round for ages looking for his old haunts and the spots that he assured me would be good. We seemed to be going round in circles getting more and more lost and I thought it was best if we gave up and went home but he insisted he knew the area,

"I used to ride my bike round here." he said.

"Your arse must have got sore." I replied.

Eventually we stopped and got out the detector. We got nothing but loud beep-beep-beeps all day but unfortunately everything we found was the same and of absolutely no interest - they were spent .303 gun cartridges - we were on an old rifle range.

I sold the metal detector years ago but something else I enjoyed and still do enjoy going to is bingo. I like the atmosphere and the people and as a bonus, sometimes I win something. I used to travel all over to different bingo halls; Brixton, Rose Hill, Kingston, Tooting, Hounslow, Kilburn, Camberwell for example. Sometimes I'd do a few in one day, getting on a train or bus to journey between them. A lot of those places used to be grand old cinemas and are very roomy inside. The one at Tooting was a Granada "Super Cinema" with a huge organ and is like a cathedral inside. Sometimes I'd just go to the local one at Sutton. It was on returning from a visit to one of these bingo afternoons that I was to experience the worst event of my life.

Joan had never been a keen bingo player and she rarely came with me. During the 1990's she had recovered from breast cancer and severe kidney stones and was now fit, but still on medication. The illnesses had left her with a heart murmur which needed daily tablets. But Joan was very careful about her health. She exercised regularly she ate all the right foods and she didn't smoke, and she didn't drink much in the way of alcohol at that time either. The cancer had gone but she was very wary now about becoming ill again and she did her best to stay in top shape. So when the tablets for her heart started causing problems leaving her tired and nauseous she had them changed and it was just a few days after this that tragedy occurred.

In September 2001 I kissed Joan goodbye as I left for my afternoon's bingo. She was sitting on the sofa reading a magazine. A couple of hours later I returned to find her in the same position - but dead. My lovely wife of over fifty years had suffered a fatal heart attack while I was out. She sat there, magazine in hand, eyes open, but head flopped forward - she was no longer with me. It was a tragic and shocking business and all I could do was phone my son Alan. "Mum's died," were the only words I could manage. He came straight over and dealt with all the necessary procedures - doctor, undertaker and later the funeral. I was in shock for many days, perhaps weeks afterwards. The day after she died I threw out all of Joan's clothes and personal items, some to the charity shop, some to the bin. I couldn't bear to have the reminders of her around me now that she herself was gone. Some time later when I was changing the bedclothes, I found one of her nighties neatly folded and positioned by her under her pillow. It sent me into a fit of tears.

The one item that I did keep was Joan's wedding ring. It had been my mother Beatrice's ring, and one day I will pass it on to one of my grandchildren for their wedding.

I stayed at the flat in Sutton, on my own, for another five years. I had a great bunch of neighbours there and even these days I still see them now and again. After being on my own for those few years I eventually felt it was time to move and so I sold it to buy a house together with my daughter Val. We live in Tolworth now with Meghan and Alex, her two children. I don't go on so many walks, I can't do the distance. I sold my car when I was in Sutton and went without for a while, but I missed it too much and now have another. I still go to bingo most days but I don't go to the horse races - the betting shops are far more comfortable, so I use those instead, occasionally. I also watch television, especially history programmes and nature programmes. We have satellite TV and there are potentially hundreds of channels available of all descriptions and twenty-four hours a day - somewhat removed from the tap dancing we listened to on the radio for entertainment all those years ago. I go to Arnhem once a year for the annual commemoration and have few weekends away in England - sometimes even Broadway. And recently I have spent a lot of time on this book - my personal memories of a life lived. I do feel privileged that I have had the time to write my life down on paper. I would love to have read similar stories from my parents and grandparents and even further back detailing the ups and downs of their lives and their hopes and dreams and how they coped with hardships and joys - but there is nothing.

The war was a big part of my life, obviously and I've been back to Arnhem over a dozen times since 1944. The first time was in the fifties with Joan. Soon after the war there was started an annual commemoration service every September for those who had been involved to attend and remember all those who had died at that time. The first service was packed with thousands of veterans, who of course were still young men then. The official military graves at Oosterbeek were marked with wooden crosses, they have now been replaced with stone memorials. It was so sad to see the names of so many men I had known all together in one graveyard. Joan and I were at that first service and stayed with a Dutch family as guests. We next went back in again in 1963 to attend the service, this time staying in Amsterdam then travelling on to Fallingbostol as I wanted to face the place where I had been imprisoned. We visited the town and that was when I went back to the jewellery shop that I had first come across when liberated from the camp. It was the same family running the business though they had different premises across the street. I bought Joan her necklace, a gold chain that by the way she subsequently lost at a reunion in Oakham!, and said hello to the family that I had encountered before. For the last few years I have been going more frequently and I've taken Alan and Val, though now of course there are less and less veterans attending and those of us left are all a lot older, although I am very impressed that it is always busy with lots of younger people remembering the past generations.

Over the years, I have spent some time tracing old friends from my regiment that I had lost touch with. Harry Sanbrook, who was one of my best mates and was with me at Stalag XI-B, went to Rhodesia after the war to work. I was trying to trace him for some time through some other friends but I finally found him by chance at a regiment reunion at Leicester. I've attended lots of these reunions over the years, at various venues, and the one at Oakham, Leiscetershire I'd been to a couple of times as that was where we did a lot of our training, but not everyone turns up to every one so I don't always see the same people. That year (it was some time in the '50s) Harry was there and I was very pleased to have found him again. We got chatting and he told me he lived in Clapham just around the corner from my wallpaper shop in Battersea Rise. It was amazing he was living on my doorstep, literally a few dozen yards away and had been there for some years and I'd been looking for him for months without any progress at all. We were certainly pleased to see each other again, it was like when we met up at the prison camp - it's always good to see an old friend. As we lived so close, we saw a lot of each other after that. He and his wife Anne would often meet up with me and Joan for a drink or two.

In the 1990's, Harry and his wife Anne, together with Joan and I all went up to see our friend Bill from the regiment who we'd recently tracked down. We went to his house and his wife directed us to his allotment where he was working. He looked so different with a long beard and stiff manner. He wasn't very talkative at all and we didn't feel very welcome. I supposed that some men would rather forget the war and all their experiences, and it was hard for him to face us and have those memories come back.

Harry died a few years ago. I went to the funeral at Kew. There weren't many of us old boys left to say goodbye, but Ken Kirkham's son was there, which I thought was nice. I also go to an Old Comrades Club at Croydon once a month. It's a meeting point for any Parachute Regiment veteran, there's blokes there who have served in the Falklands, Egypt, Korea, Iraq, Afghanistan - all over, and although there aren't many as old as me, there *are* a few and I'm not the only one from Arnhem, there's still a few of us left! I always attend the November Poppy day parade in Croydon with them. Croydon is where I spent my teenage years and funnily enough it has been twinned with Arnhem. Joan and I used to meet up with Harry McKenzie and his girlfriend there (this Harry was my platoon commander) and sometimes we'd see another mate of mine, Alfie Freeman as well as another Bill, who it turned out had been in Stalag XI B with me though I hadn't known him at the time. Bill had suffered a terrible gunshot injury to his stomach and had been badly patched up afterwards. For the whole of his imprisonment in Germany he hadn't been able to stand up straight. He'd had further operations on his return to England and thankfully was sorted out.

More recently I went to a memorial service for Colonel Smyth, which had been organized by his daughter and was held at Eastbourne. Also, just three years ago one of the 10th Battalion members died and left some money in his will to be shared out amongst all of us still here - there were twenty-two of us at the time and we felt honoured to be remembered and thought of by him. I've also appeared on a Channel 4 television documentary about some youngsters training to do parachute jumps - I was interviewed as a veteran about my real-life experiences along with some other men, and I've been in local papers a few times over the years.

The battle at Arnhem will not be forgotten for a long time, it affected so many lives.

****

There is just one important episode of my life that has not yet been told - tracking down my birth parents. In 1921 a young couple were ready to throw their newborn son into a river so that they could get on with their lives without the burden of a child. That couple were my mother and father - Marie and Lewis Bench. After my dad, Edwin died, in the early 1960s I finally felt ready to confront the past. Of course, I was parted from the Benches on the day I was born and had only a moment with my natural mother and if I ever looked into her eyes, I remembered nothing. I knew that both she and my father would be strangers to me and yet I still had an urge to meet them, perhaps get to know them. Dad had lost contact with them when they had travelled to America and all I had were a few letters and some memories from Dad from years ago.

I knew from my birth certificate that my father's name was John Lewis Bench, and that he had come from Birmingham. Bench is not a common name, and in the sixties, this urge to trace my roots would sometimes find me browsing through the telephone directories at the local library looking up the Benches and seeing if there were any with the initials 'J. L.' In the sixties, all

177

telephone owners had a local telephone directory delivered to their home each year and there was always a wider selection of directories in phone boxes and a complete set, covering the whole country, at libraries. The directories listed everyone with a phone and would show their surname, initials and address, unless that person had specifically requested to the telephone company not to be included, but in those days nearly every one was listed, hardly anybody went 'ex-directory'. I would often pop into a library, either near home or work or sometimes when out shopping and would take down one of the Birmingham books and flick through looking for my father's name. (Telephone listings were most likely to be under the name of the man of the house so I never looked for Marie's initials.) My attempts had never been completely serious, because I could have just phoned up directory enquiries which was a free operator controlled service who could look up the number for you for any part of Great Britain, and anyway, I knew that the Benches had moved to America and could well still be there. I was just curious. One day, I happened to be in Sutton and popped into the library there to have a quick browse. I pulled down one of the Birmingham area books, turned to the 'B's' and not only did I actually find a 'Bench' but I found a 'J. L. Bench'. He lived in Egbaston, on the south west side of Birmingham. I wrote down the number, took it home, stewed on it for a while and then I phoned him.

A woman answered. Looking back, I suppose this could have been my mother, but strangely, I never considered that issue, I was too focused on the name John Lewis Bench. I asked for him, explaining that I was trying to trace a relative who was from Smethwick. The lady who had answered the phone was Hilda Bench, Lewis's second wife. As I explained that it was my father who I was looking for and told her the year and place of my birth she said,

"Must be my old man then."

She obviously knew some details about my circumstances of adoption already, as before she went to fetch him she said,

"You don't feel any umbrage do you?"

"No," I said, "I don't have any grudges, just an interest in speaking to him."

Lewis came on the line. It's hard to remember any emotion. We chatted about my work, the wallpaper shops, and his job - he was working as a porter in a laboratory at the nearby University, and eventually we agreed it would be good to meet. First we exchanged photos by mail and then a few days later, Joan and I drove the 130 miles from New Malden to Nursery Close, Harbourne at Egbaston in Birmingham on the newly constructed M1 motorway.

I found out a lot about my father's present life and a little about his past but the day of my birth was never spoken of. Neither of us could bring ourselves to discuss the matter and I don't suppose it would have done any good - after all, I had had a great childhood, no harm had come to me and here I was, alive and well over forty years later, married with three children and doing well. I didn't think any good would have come from digging up bad memories and so we left them buried.

John Lewis Bench, my biological father

Lewis was happily re-settled in Birmingham, close to where he had been brought up. He was married to Hilda, who was a lovely woman, very kind and friendly and she worked for Birmingham council - looking after abandoned children. How uncanny is that?! Lewis was still a good pianist, despite developing arthritis, and he still played professionally in a local club. He had a piano in his house and he played for me. It was marvellous to hear and I wished I had practised harder for my own music lessons all those years ago - the potential competence as a pianist is certainly in the genes as my own grandson Alex has a talent too.

I visited Lewis a few times over the next couple of years, I even met a couple of distant cousins. Joan came sometimes, but Alan, Valerie and Derek never met him. Lewis had kept in touch with my mother Marie, even after their divorce and he told me that she was still in the United States. He also told me that neither of them had ever tried to trace me which should have been a bit of a blow, another rejection, but I wasn't really all that bothered. We didn't communicate particularly regularly, I felt that the itch had been scratched and there was nothing more to find out. After the initial meetings, we went without contact for a year or so until he phoned me up one day to say that Marie was coming back from America, and asked if I'd like to meet her.

Marie had recently been widowed and she could not afford to live by herself in America and so she was coming to Weston-Super-Mare where she had a sister. (She actually fell out with her sister after a while and rented some rooms by herself above a shop.) Lewis and a mutual friend of their's got in touch with her once she arrived in England and it was arranged that I would go to see her. Joan and I travelled to Cheltenham station where we picked up Lewis and his friend, they'd come on the train from Birmingham, and we all travelled on to see Marie together - the only time that Lewis, Marie and their son Colin (me) were ever reunited.

Marie said that she was very pleased to see me and had often thought about me over the years. Perhaps she had. After all, giving your baby away is not something that is easily forgotten. However, I didn't feel that her words were spoken naturally and it wasn't just that they were said with an unfamiliar American accent - it seemed more like lines than sentiment, but then she was an actress and a failed one at that. Of course, it can be expected that I would be bitter, but I didn't feel it. I was happy to forget the past and get to know her. I bought her a television set when she moved to her new rooms and I invited her to my house in New Malden to visit her grandchildren. She came on the train from Weston-Super-Mare and I picked her up at Paddington to stay with us for a couple of weeks. I took her to the local sights and shops, to Richmond Park, she met my friends, saw where I worked. She told me a lot about her life in America and her second husband, his nursery business and her friends and what a wonderful time she had had. She was confident and chatty. I don't remember her asking me much about my past.

After Marie visited us, we kept in touch and I visited her maybe a dozen times more. (I was even inspired to trace other members of my family and started a folder where I kept copies of birth, marriage and death certificates going back nearly 200 years. I made many trips to the records office, contacted a few distant cousins and drew up a family tree.)

When we had the guesthouse in Broadway, I visited from there a couple of times and when I lived in Sutton I visited from there too. Marie and I never became the 'best of friends', we weren't even close. But what can be expected after nearly fifty years apart? I suppose that meeting again at all had defied all likely probabilities.

Meeting Marie, my biological mother

On the occasions that I was with her, which when added together was quite a brief period really, sometimes the brash front would come down and Marie was quite emotional for a moment or two and then her eyes would fill with tears - though none ever fell. Maybe there *was* some regret there after all. I would look away and she would compose herself once more.

Eventually my mother became frail and moved to an Old

People's home, where she died in 1988. I did not attend her funeral. I'd seen my *true* mother buried when I was twelve years old.

****

Sometimes people have told me how brave I was to have coped with all the misfortunes in my life - from my abandonment at birth, the death of my adoptive mother, being shot at Arnhem and imprisoned for six months nearly starving to death and then the loss of my wife Joan, but I certainly never feel brave. These things just happened to me and I coped as best I could with each situation. I prefer to look on the positive aspects of each incident and consider myself a lucky man. For example, I was saved from an early death as a baby by a passing postman, I had a wonderful childhood in the Cotswolds with a loving mother, who was after all only mortal but in our time together she gave me a marvellous start to my life, and my bullet wound at Arnhem probably saved me from being killed on the front line. My life in the prison camp taught me not to take anything for granted - not even the basic necessities such as clean water, warmth and food and through my grim life in the Forest of Dean at least I learnt a trade which I was able to apply to my own successful businesses in later years. To cap all this, I also had over fifty years living with a wonderful wife which is more than a lot of men can claim, and we had three children all healthy and happy. I'm now enjoying my retirement and very much glad that I'm still here!

All in all I'm quite content with my lot!

Me with my three children and four grandchildren

"Dropped In It" - Glossary of terms

AWOL - absent without leave, i.e. taking time off without permission - a punishable offence taken very seriously by the military

BARRAGE BALLOON - a large gas filled balloon tethered to the ground by metal cables - mostly used as a defence against low flying aircraft

BILLY BUNTER - is a fictional character created by Charles Hamilton (pen name Frank Richards) at the also fictional Greyfriars School

COFFIN FURNITURE - the metal fittings such as handles and crosses that go on the outside of a coffin

CO-OP - Co-operative shop where local food producers can obtain a fair price for their produce

DDT - an abbreviation of **d**ichloro**d**iphenyl**t**richloroethane, it is a synthetic pesticide

DHSS - Department of Health and Social Security (Government body in charge of benefits)

DIVVI - dividend stamps issued by the co-op for loyalty to their store and collected on a card to be traded in for goods once full

DOGFIGHTS – a form of aerial combat between fighter aircraft

DRIPPING - the saved fat from a cooked joint of meat

FRIENDLY FIRE - to receive friendly fire would mean that you were accidentally under attack from your own side

GUINEA - One pound and one shilling (expensive items were often priced in Guineas to make it sound less)

HI-DE-HI - a television comedy show made in the 1980s based on life in a British holiday camp of the 1950s

LDV - Local Defence Volunteers, local defence team comprising of volunteers ineligible for the regular army, usually due to age - hence the term "Dad's Army"

MANGLE-WURZLE - a root vegetable primarily used as animal fodder

M & B - May & Baker - a British chemical company who manufactured tablets for fighting infection (which were apparently very inefficient and had the side effect of causing depression)

NAAFI - Navy, Army and Air Force Institutes, official trading organization of HM Forces providing retail and leisure services to the services.

RASC - Royal Army Service Corp - a corps of the British Army responsible for transport of food, fuel, water and domestic stores as well as personnel (they had the nickname of "Run Away,

Someone's Coming")

POW - prisoner of war - a person held prisoner by the opposing side (enemy) during wartime

SHRAPNEL - metal fragments from an exploded bomb or artillery shell

TA - see Territorial Army

TEAS-MADE - an electrical appliance consisting of alarm clock and kettle which prepares a brewed pot of tea to wake up to

TERRITORIAL ARMY - volunteer reserve force of regular army, part-time only but still paid

WAAF – Women's Auxillary Air Force

WINGS - badge resembling wings, an official symbol of parachute regiment

Postscript:
Since completing this book, I have learnt, from a reader, some more details about my friend Tommy Farrage who was killed during 'Operation Market Garden' in 1944. I have been informed that he was shot in the spine during the battles soon after landing and he died from his wounds. He was buried in an unmarked grave in Holland.

1451593R0

Printed in Great Britain by
Amazon.co.uk, Ltd.,
Marston Gate.